MW01132069

The Holy Sabbath

by

Arthur Pink

(1886-1952)

Published 2014 by Classic Domain Publishing

ISBN-13: 978-1500808709

ISBN-10: 1500808709

Note From The Editor Of Classic Domain Publishing:

Keeping the Lord's Day holy is obeying the 4th of the 10 commandments, which are commandments and not suggestions. And as Jesus states they are here until Heaven and Earth pass away (Matt 5:17-20). The church from the Book of Acts time gathered on the first day of the week, the day Jesus was resurrected, calling it the "Lord's Day" and set it aside as their sabbath – 1 Cor 16:1-2, Acts 20:7 & Rev 1:9, keeping it holy and wholly for God in worship, giving, Bible study, church, prayer, evangelising (and not for worldly things, sports, restaurants, shopping, TV etc). This is a most neglected command today, but it was not neglected in church history. Many of the greatest revivalists and reformers in Church history preached and kept the Lord's Day holy such as: John Wesley, DL Moody, Charles Spurgeon, David Livingston, William Wilberforce, Hudson Taylor, Charles Finney, William Booth, George Whitfield and many others who have massively impacted the church. In fact during times of revival it is highly significant that revivals where always accompanied by a renewal and revival of keeping the sabbath day (the Lord's day) as well.

TABLE OF CONTENTS

PREFACE

"This is the day which the LORD hath made," and therefore it is peculiarly and pre-eminently "the Lord's Day," and so it is expressly denominated in Revelation 1:10. It is the day which the Lord made specially for this Christian dispensation, namely, the first of the week. It is the day which has been made forever memorable by loosing the Redeemer from the pains of death. It is now the day in which His people are to celebrate the Saviour's victory over the sepulchre. And therefore Christians must exclaim, "we will rejoice and be glad in it": not only because of its appointment, but because of its occasion, for Christ's resurrection was both for His own honour and for our salvation. Holy mirth, then, should fill our hearts at this season: Sabbath Days ought to be unto us as foretastes of Heaven itself. Then let us welcome each weekly return of it, and duly tune our hearts to show forth His praises therein.—A.W.P.

INTRODUCTION

Two things are absolutely essential for the maintenance of vital godliness: the profession of its truth and the practice or exercise of its power, for they mutually assist each other. Where there is no profession of faith in its truth, none will express its power in obedience; and without obedience, profession is worthless. Clearly is this exemplified in connection with the Holy Sabbath. In proportion as the pulpit has failed to insist on and press the claims of the Sacred Day, vital godliness has been weakened and all but destroyed, and commensurate with the growth of an empty profession has been the decay of genuine piety. Things have now come to such a deplorable state that we may well exclaim, "Truth is fallen in the street" (Isa. 59:14), yea, is being ruthlessly trampled under foot not only by the masses in general but also by the great majority of those in high places. It is therefore incumbent upon all who fear and love God to do whatever lies within their power to rescue the Sabbath from its present profanation.

Whatever furnishes help, according to the revealed will of God, in the promotion of good works, is greatly to be valued, especially so in a time when the profession of the Truth is being so widely called into question, and its practice not only neglected but despised. Now nothing is so well calculated to accomplish this end than the solemn observance of a weekly day of rest, hallowed unto God, for that lies at the very foundation of all true piety. Rightly did John Owen affirm, "Amongst all the outward means of conveying to the present generation that rule which was at first taught and delivered by Jesus Christ and His Apostles, there hath been none more effectual than the universal uninterrupted observance of such a day for the celebration of the religious worship appointed in the Gospel. The profession of our Christian religion in the world at this day doth depend upon it. How much it tends to the exercise and expression of the power of religion cannot but be evident to all, unless they be such as hate it."-The Lord's Day has ever been a precious boon to all genuine Christians.

Occupied as most of them are with worldly concerns during the remainder of the week, they feel that but for this merciful restraint of one day in seven devoted to the worship and service of God, they would soon become wholly absorbed in the things of time and sense. But the Sabbath and its holy exercises restores the claims of God to an ascendance over their minds. On this day they are led to examine their spiritual progress, reflect upon their duties, meditate on the grand truths of Divine revelation, and prepare for eternity. By faithfully discharging the obligations of this Sacred Day their souls are cleansed from the defilement contracted during the week, their affections raised unto things above, and new strength is obtained for the engagements which lie before them. Christians generally know full well that they owe much of their growth in grace to the blessings of the Sabbath.

Again—attention should be called to the vast amount of benevolent Christian effort which has resulted from the instrumentality of the Sabbath. It has been pertinently pointed out, "If all those who have to secure their livelihood by bodily or mental exertion were obliged to labour through seven days of the week as they now labour through six of them, how few would have time or strength to visit the poor, to teach the young, or to speak of Christ to the ungodly! But through this ordinance of the Sabbath hundreds of thousands of persons in this country, who devote six days to hard labour, bodily or mentally, give a part of their Sabbath to the religious instruction of the young and ignorant. Without the Sabbath, nearly all the inappreciable good which is now done by Sabbath Schools, and much of that which attends the visiting of the sick and distressed in cities, would vanish from the land" (W. B. Noel).

"The Sabbath was made for man": God has graciously sanctified it for the good of the whole world. It is highly probable that more persons are converted to the Lord on that day than all the other six together. When anyone is awakened to a concern about his soul, he naturally looks forward to the return of that time when he can most successfully seek his spiritual good. Moreover, how many there are who, though not earnestly inquiring after God, yet attend public worship, and there learn much of the letter of Scripture and acquire some respect for its authority, who otherwise would grow up as heathens. Furthermore, since the Sabbath alone releases hundreds of the disciples of Christ from secular labours to employ a part of their energies in the instructing of the ignorant, who can say how much of the religious knowledge and moral principle which still exists in our nation, is instrumentally due to the institution of this Sacred Rest? Godliness has never flourished in the world from its foundation till now, nor will it ever do so, without a due attendance upon this Divine ordinance, and it requires very little perspicuity to foresee what increasing disorder and disaster will yet ensue if it be totally disregarded. It is an incontestable fact that the times when the Sabbath's sanctity was most faithfully proclaimed and maintained in the British Isles—and we may add, in the U.S.A.—were those in which true spirituality was healthiest and vital godliness was in its most flourishing state. The men to whom, under God, we owe this, are the ones whose writings are still among the most precious treasures of English religious literature. A right observance of the Lord's Day lies at the foundation of national happiness and prosperity. So prolific of good is this blessed day that its powerful influences on the well-being of our country vitally affects its spiritual intelligence, the morality of its social order, and the liberties of its people.

So far, then, from the Sabbath law being a heavy burden which God has laid on His creatures, it is a noble boon and an inestimable blessing. So far from it being an unkind deprivation of our liberty, its right observance makes for an entrance into real spiritual freedom. "God blessed the seventh day" (Gen. 2:3). The Sabbath was Divinely designed, from its original institution, to be a day of blessing to all who duly observed it. Therefore has the Lord declared, "Blessed is the man that keepeth the Sabbath from polluting it" (Isa. 56:2): it is not a day of irksome restraint, but one of peace and good. It is a gracious gift whereby, in the midst of our toils, we are granted a deliverance even from that curse, "in the sweat of thy face shalt thou eat bread, till thou return unto the ground" (Gen. 3:19). Man's Maker has mercifully secured to him one seventh portion of his whole life wherein he may rest his wearied body and refresh his needy soul, by separating himself from the toil of this life and fixing his contemplation on the life to come.

The great excellence of this Divine grant lies not, as many seem to suppose, in a mere bodily blessing, appointed for the recuperation of our physical frame—that is but a secondary object; no, the abstention from mental and manual labours is not its primary use and purpose but is only preparatory to its great and chief design. The high and prime value of it lies in the salvation and sanctification of God's people, who experience growth in grace and in the knowledge of the Lord by obeying His Law and keeping faithfully His Sabbaths. As a means of grace towards our sanctification, none, under the blessing of God, is more effectual than the Sabbath. Our right observance thereof has the fullest assurance of that promise, "them that honour Me, I will honour." Our happiness lies in the favour and service of God; that favour is "life" and that service is "perfect freedom." Then let us do all that lies within our power—by precept, example, and encouragement—to maintain the claims of God's own day.

It lies not within the capacity of any mortal to adequately set forth the tremendous value and supreme moment of a Scriptural observance of the Holy Sabbath. Let us briefly call attention to a few features wherein and whereby the Holy Spirit has emphasized the fundamental importance of this Divine institution. It is placed on virtually the frontispiece of Divine revelation, for immediately after the account of creation we are informed that God Himself rested on that day and hallowed it. It was the very first lesson taught the children of Israel in the wilderness, impressed upon them by the Lord's withholding a supply of manna on that day (Exo. 16). It was made the outstanding "sign" between Jehovah and His people (Exo. 31:13). The most fearful judgments were sent upon them for their violation of the Fourth Commandment. The Lord Jesus set His imprimatur upon it in an unmistakable manner (Luke 4:16). Finally, the Spirit Himself placed special stress upon this holy ordinance by communicating the last book of Scripture to John on that day (Rev. 1:10).

To be guilty of desecrating the Holy Sabbath is therefore no light matter, my reader. The violation of the Fourth Commandment is a sin of the gravest and blackest kind; yet, sad to say, the profanation of the Lord's Day has become one of the most common crimes of our perverse generation. So general is its pollution that few have any conscience on the matter, but placidly take it as a matter of course. The world has turned the Holy Day into a holiday, and even the majority of professing Christians join hands with them therein. No wonder God is displeased with us as a people, and is more and more evidencing His displeasure against us. Britain has disturbed God's rest, and He is now disturbing Britain's rest; and unless we repent of and forsake this sin as a Nation, then we are most certainly treasuring up to ourselves wrath against the day of wrath.

Fully assured that the sanctification of the Sabbath is indispensable for the promotion of the manifestative glory of God, the health and prosperity of His people, the salvation of sinners, and the national well-being—firmly convinced that the desecration of this Blessed Day is our greatest and most grievous national sin, on account of which the Lord is visiting us with judgment, which ominously threatens to become far more severe unless we mend our ways—this writer dares not remain silent thereon, but determines to use whatever influence he possesses in pressing the claims of this sacred and grand institution. Then let all who fear the Lord, who dread His displeasure, who desire to see a revival of vital godliness in the churches, and who love their country and wish to save it from being completely paganized, resolve and determine, "as for me and my house," we will "remember the Sabbath Day to keep it holy."

If the Sabbath were of little or no value, there would be some excuse for standing by and leaving it to its assailants. But since it is of Divine appointment, since its weighty and venerable claims are as binding on us today as they were upon God's people in Old Testament times, since the Lord is very jealous of its sanctity (honouring the nation which respects it and visiting His indignation upon those who pollute it), since its proper observance is fraught with such spiritual blessing to the churches and moral and temporal good to the country, then we should do no less than evidence an uncompromising firmness, yet reasonable and enlightened zeal, in doing all we can to preserve this imperiled treasure, and thus secure for future generations a boon won for ourselves by the efforts, sacrifices, and prayers of godly progenitors. Thus did our forefathers, and woe be unto as if we now squander our birthright.

In view of all that has been pointed out above, is it not tragic beyond words to witness not only the general indifference of the vast majority of professing Christians unto the claims of the Holy Sabbath and to the world's awful profanation of it, but also to find that many influential men among the reputedly orthodox sections of Christendom —the "leaders of Christian thought"—should oppose those who are striving for the preservation of this spiritual heritage? These men are seeking to destroy its very foundations by teaching that the Sabbath is only a Jewish institution, and therefore is not binding upon us today. Unspeakably sad is it to find some whom we must regard as brethren in Christ, and who are standing firmly for the Divine inspiration and authority of the Scriptures, yet in this vital matter making common cause with the Lord's enemies.

John Owen commenced his exercitations on the Day of Sacred Rest by citing, "God hath made man upright, but they have sought out many inventions" (Eccl. 7:29), adding, "The truth hereof we also find by woeful

ARTHUR W. PINK

experience, not only in sundry particular instances, but in the whole course of men in this world, and in all their concerns with respect to God. There is not anything wherein and whereabouts they have not found out many inventions, to the disturbance and perverting of that state of peace and quietness wherein all things were made of God . . . An evident instance we have hereof in the business of a day of sacred rest and the worship of God therein required."

If this justly renowned Puritan had cause to complain in his time at the many controversies which had been raised about this Divine institution, "agitating among men of all sorts," and who grieved over their inventions, "to our own disturbance and to the perverting of the right ways of God," we wonder how he would feel could he take a survey of the present situation. O what "inventions" have professing Christians resorted to in their efforts to set aside the Holy Sabbath, inventions which have greatly influenced the minds of multitudes and enervated them in the practice of that piety which the Lord's Day inculcates and stimulates. How happy Satan must be when he succeeds in moving "Bible teachers" to affirm that the Sabbath is not for us. It is Christ being again wounded in the house of His friends.

Such opposition to the Sabbath is a challenge to all who prize and revere it. The more it be opposed by assailants, the more firmly and unitedly must its lovers rise up in its defense. When some would set aside the Sabbath as a day of rest and worship on the ground of our being under a more spiritual dispensation, we must show the utter fallacy of such an absurd conclusion. Is the secularization of the Sabbath more befitting a spiritual dispensation then the religious observance of it!—more calculated to promote vital godliness than the dedication of it to holy exercises and attendance on the means of grace? The question answers itself. Then if you, my reader, love the Sabbath because you have found that its devout and dutiful employment has brought you many blessings, it is your bounden duty to spread the knowledge of its claims throughout the land. Pray that it may please the Lord to bless this humble effort to such an end.

1. ITS INSTITUTION

"And on the seventh day God ended His work which He had made; and He rested on the seventh day from His work which He had made. And God blessed the seventh day and sanctified it: because that in it He had rested from all His work which God created and made" (Gen. 2:2, 3). Before commenting upon these verses perhaps it is well to make a few preliminary remarks thereon. First, let us point out how emphatically they repudiate the error of those who declare that the Sabbath was an institution peculiar to the Jews. More than 2,000 years before the Lord entered into covenant with them at Sinai, the weekly day of sacred rest was appointed and consecrated by the Creator. Instead of its origin dating only from the time when the Ten Commandments were written on the tables of stone, its inception carries us right back to the very beginning of history. As we shall see (D.V.) when we come to examine Exodus 20, the Lord Himself there declared the Sabbath was as old as the world itself.

Not only is it a glaring mistake to suppose the Sabbath was first instituted at Sinai, but it is equally wrong to insist that it is binding on Jews only. The reasons which Jehovah gave in Exodus 20:8-11 why the Sacred Day must be observed are just as pertinent to and incontestable for the Gentiles as they are for the Jews: the original occasion of its appointment and the design thereof hold good with equal respect for the entire human race. Nor is this any arbitrary assertion of ours. Nothing could be plainer than the words of our Redeemer: "the Sabbath was made for man" (Mark 2:27) and not merely for one small fraction of mankind. "The weekly day of rest is one of two things that were ordained in and have come from a sinless Eden. The Sabbath was before Moses, before Abraham—the only other relic of the primitive Paradise is marriage—ideal marriage. As well make marriage a matter of Mosaic legislation as the Sabbath law, since both of them were instituted and ordained for man in Eden" (A. T. Pierson).

But plain though the above considerations are to any unprejudiced and simple reader of the Scriptures, there are those who raise cavils against them. Unwilling, at any price, to admit the Sabbath is binding on us today, various subterfuges have been resorted to in an endeavour to set aside the obvious meaning of Genesis 2:2, 3. Some have argued, "it only seems to import that the Sabbath was then instituted," making out that this passage is to be understood only as giving "the reason of that particular day being chosen, not that it was then actually appointed and set apart." To say that these verses contain merely an anticipation of the Fourth Commandment is handling the Word of God deceitfully. Those verses are the continuation of a plain historical narrative. Having finished the account of the creation of the world in the first chapter of Genesis, and given a recapitulation of it in 2:1, Moses declared what immediately followed thereon, namely, the rest of God on the seventh day and His blessing and sanctifying of that day.

For the special benefit of those who have sadly misrepresented the teaching of Calvin on this subject, we give a brief quotation from the remarks of that renowned Reformer and expositor on this passage: "That blessing of the seventh day is nothing else than the solemn consecration of it; by virtue of which God claims for Himself on that day the labours and occupations of men. It is, indeed, the proper study of their whole life to be exercised in considering the infinite goodness, justice, power, and wisdom of God, as displayed on the vast theater of Heaven and earth; but, lest men should apply less diligently to this than they ought, every seventh day was peculiarly set apart. God, therefore, first rested; then He blessed that rest, that it might be sacred among men through all coming ages; He consecrated each seventh day to rest, that His own example might furnish the perpetual rule. Not that God simply enjoined men to take their leisure every seventh day, as if He delighted in idleness; but that, being released from all business, they might with more freedom employ their minds on the Creator of the world—His own example stimulating them to the duty, and engaging them to its performance."

Others have sought to base an argument on the fact that the actual word "Sabbath" is not found in Genesis 2:2, 3—but how futile is such a cavil may at once be seen by a reference to Exodus 20. When it pleased the Lord God to assume the immediate government over the people of Israel at Sinai, He not only restored the Sabbath to its original place of honour, but did so by recognizing it as an existing ordinance, re-enforcing a creation-institution. In referring back to Genesis 2, Jehovah expressly termed that first seventh day the Sabbath: "For in six days the Lord made Heaven and earth, the sea and all that in them is, and rested the seventh day, wherefore the Lord blessed the Sabbath Day and hallowed it." We will not waste any further time and space by considering other objections which the perversity and unbelief of man have brought against this simple passage. The 2nd chapter of Genesis opens with the words, "Thus the heavens and the earth were finished, and all the host of them." And then the very next thing we read of is the institution of the Sabbath rest. Thus, to appoint and sanctify the Sabbath was God's first act after the earth had been made fit for human habitation. Nothing could more emphatically press upon us the fundamental importance of this Divine ordinance, and the priority of its claims upon us—claims to which every consideration of selfish interests must be strictly subordinated. "The weekly Sabbath, therefore, is the first institution of God, and bears on its very origin the stamp of a universal and perpetual appointment: good for man even when surrounded by the glories of Paradise that is lost—and much more so now, when called to struggle and prepare for the higher glories of the Paradise that is to be won" (P. Fairbairn).

Four things call for special consideration in the passage now before us. 1. The primal Sabbath was a rest day. Emphasis is laid upon this feature by the repetition in thought which is found in the two parts of Genesis 2:2. First, on the seventh day, "God ended His work which He had made." Second, "and He rested on the seventh day from all His work He had made." Therefore the prime element and basic truth connected with the

Sabbath is rest. Before raising the question as to why God "rested," let us offer a few remarks on the nature of His rest.

It has been said repeatedly by a certain class of expositors that this rest of God consisted of His satisfaction in the work of His hands, that it was God looking out in complacency over His fair creation. But, we are told, that this "rest" of God did not last for long: it was rudely broken by the entrance of sin, and ever since man fell God has been "working"—John 5:17 being appealed to in proof. That such a definition of the "rest" of God in Genesis 2:2 should have been received by a large number of the Lord's people, only goes to show how few of them ever do much thinking or studying for themselves. It also proves how the most puerile interpretations of Scripture are likely to be accepted, if they are made by reputable teachers, who on other matters are worthy of respect. Finally, it demonstrates what a real need there is for each of us to humbly, prayerfully, and diligently bring everything we read and hear to a rigid examination in the light of Holy Scripture.

That God's "rest" in Genesis 2:2 was not the complacence of the Creator prior to the entrance of sin, is unequivocally evidenced by the fact that Satan had fallen before the time contemplated in that verse. How could God look abroad upon creation with Divine contentment when the highest creature of all had become the blackest and basest of sinners? How could God find satisfaction in all the works of His hands when the anointed cherub had apostatised, and in his rebellion had dragged down with him "the third part" of the angels (Rev. 12:4)? No, this is manifestly untenable. Some other definition of God's "rest" must therefore be sought.

Now we need to pay very close attention to the exact wording here, as everywhere. Genesis 2:2 does not say (nor does Exo. 20:10) that God rested from all work, for that was not true. Genesis 2:2 is careful to say, "on the seventh day God ended His work which He had made," and, "He rested on the seventh day from all His work which He had made." And this

16

brings out and calls attention to the basic feature and primal element in the Sabbath: it is a resting from the activities commonly pursued during the six working days. But the Sabbath Day is not appointed as a day for the cessation of all activities —to remain in bed and sleep through that day would not be spending the Sabbath as God requires it to be spent. What particular works are required and are permissible, we shall (D.V.) show later; but what we would now press upon the reader is the fact that, according to Genesis 2:2 the Sabbath rest consists of ceasing from the labours of the working week.

Genesis 2:2 does not state that on the seventh day God did no work, for, as we have seen, that would not have been true. God did work on the seventh day, though His activities on that day were of a different nature from the ones in which He had been engaged during the preceding days. And herein we see not only the marvellous accuracy of Scripture, but the perfect example God set before His people, for as we shall yet show, there are works suited to the Sabbath. For God to have ceased from all works on that first seventh day in human history, would have meant the total destruction of all creation. God's providential workings could not cease, or no provision would be made for the supply of His creatures' wants. "All things" needed to be "upheld" or they would have passed into non-entity.

Let us fix it firmly in our minds that rest is not inertia. The Lord Jesus has entered into "rest" (Heb. 4:10), yet is He not inactive, for He ever lives to make intercession. And when the saints shall enter their eternal rest, they shall not be inactive, for it is written, "And His servants shall serve Him" (Rev. 22:3). So here with God. His rest on that first Sabbath Day was not a rest of total inactivity. He rested from the work of creation and restoration, but He then began (and has never ceased) the work of Providence—the providing of supplies for His myriad creatures.

But now the question arises, why did God rest on the seventh day? Why did He so order it that all the works recorded in Genesis 1 were completed

17

in six days, and that then He rested? Certainly it was not because the Creator needed rest, for, "the Creator of the ends of the earth fainteth not, neither is weary" (Isa. 40:28). Why, then, did He "rest," and why is it so recorded on the top of the second page of Holy Writ? Surely there can be only one answer: as an example for man! Nor is this answer merely a logical or plausible inference of ours. It rests on Divine authority. It is based directly upon the words of none other than the Son of God, for He expressly declared, "The Sabbath was made for man" (Mark 2:27): made not for God, but for man. Nothing could be plainer, nothing simpler, nothing more unequivocal.

2. The next thing that we would carefully note in this initial reference to the Sabbath is that Genesis 2:3 tells us this day was blessed by God: "and God blessed the seventh day." The reason why God blessed the seventh day was not because it was the seventh, but because, "in it He had rested." Hence, when the Sabbath law was written upon the tables of stone, God did not say, "Remember the seventh to keep it holy," but "Remember the Sabbath Day to keep it holy." And again, He did not say, "He blessed the seventh day and hallowed it," but, "He blessed the Sabbath Day and hallowed it."

But why should He do so? Why single out the seventh day thus? Young's Concordance defines the Hebrew word for "blessed" here as "to declare blessed." But why should God have "declared" the seventh day blessed? for there is no hint that He pronounced any of the other days blessed. Surely it was not for the mere day's sake. Only one other alternative remains: God declared the seventh day blessed because it was the Sabbath Day, and because He would have every reader of His Word know, right at the beginning, that special Divine blessing marks its observance. This at once refutes a modern heresy and removes an aspersion which many cast upon God. The Sabbath was not appointed to bring man into bondage. It was not designed to be a burden, but a blessing! And if history demonstrates anything, it demonstrates beyond all room for doubt that the family or nation which has kept the Sabbath Day holy, has been markedly blessed of God; and contrariwise, that the family or nation which has desecrated the Sabbath, has been cursed of God. Explain it as we may, the fact remains.

3. Genesis 2:3 teaches us that the Sabbath was a day set apart for sacred use. This comes out plainly in the words, "And God blessed the seventh day and sanctified it," or as the R.V. has it, "God blessed the seventh day and hallowed it." The prime meaning (according to its Scriptural usage) of the Hebrew word rendered "sanctified" or "hallowed" is to set apart for sacred use. This shows plainly that here in Genesis 2:3 we have something more than an historical reference to the rest of God on the seventh day, and even something more than God setting an example before His creatures. The fact that we are told God "sanctified" it, proves conclusively that here we have the original institution of the Sabbath, the Divine appointment of it for man's use and observance. As exemplified by the Creator Himself, the Sabbath Day is separated from the six preceding days of manual labour.

4. Let us call attention to a notable omission in Genesis 2:3. If the reader will turn to Genesis 1 he will find that at the close of each of the six working days the Holy Spirit says, "and the evening and the morning were," etc.: see Genesis 1:5, 8, 13, 19, 23, 31. But here in Genesis 2:2, 3 we do not read, "and the evening and the morning were the seventh day"; nor are we told what took place on the eighth day. In other words, the Holy Spirit has not mentioned the ending of the "seventh day." Why is this? There is a reason for every omission in Scripture, a Divine reason; and there is a reason why the Holy Spirit omitted the usual formula at the close of the seventh day. We suggest that this omission is a silent but most significant intimation that the observance of the Sabbath never would end—it was to be perpetuated as long as time should last!

In conclusion it should be pointed out that Genesis 2 contains nothing whatever which enables us to determine which day of our week this primal "seventh day" was. We have absolutely no means of knowing whether that original seventh day fell on a Saturday, a Sunday, or any other day of the week—for the simple reason that we are quite unable to ascertain on which day that first week began. All we do know, and all which it is necessary for us to know is, that the seventh day was the day which followed six days of manual work. As to which day of the week is the Christian Sabbath we shall (D.V.) consider later.

2. ITS HISTORY

In our examination of the original institution of the Holy Sabbath we pondered the three acts of the Creator as recorded in Genesis 2:3, each of which had distinct and special reference to man. First, God "rested on the seventh day," thereby giving an example for us to follow. But this was not left to be vaguely inferred, for second, "God blessed the seventh day," setting on it a special dowry for all who should give due heed to its proper end and object. "What men may lose for the moment in productive employment, shall be amply compensated by the refreshment it will bring to his frame—by the enlargement and elevation of his soul—above all, by the spiritual fellowship and interest in God which becomes the abiding portion of those who follow Him in their ways, and perpetually return to Him as the supreme rest of their souls" (P. Fairbairn). Third, God "sanctified it," setting it sacredly apart from the other six days, thus conferring on it a distinctive character.

But in their efforts to evade the obvious force of Genesis 2:3 some have raised the objection that Genesis 2 records no express command for man to keep the Sabbath. Really, such a cavil is undeserving of notice, yet as a few readers are disturbed by it, we will briefly answer the objection. First, it is plainly required of us in and by the law of nature that some part of our time (Divinely given to us) should be set apart and devoted to God, for the solemn observance of His worship in the world. And where but in Genesis 2:3 could primitive man learn which part of that time was to be thus employed? That natural dictate is met by the Sabbath law requiring us to sanctify one day in seven. Second, this pretense of any obscurity that is in the command of Genesis 2:3 is easily removed by another instance of like antiquity. It has been universally acknowledged that a promise of Christ was given in Genesis 3:15 for the faith of the ancients, yet that very verse was addressed to the Serpent in the form of a curse! With equal propriety, then, could we deny any promise in Genesis 3:15 and declare there is no command in Genesis 2:3—each is self-evidently implied.

Third, a yet more decisive consideration is found in our Lord's words, "the Sabbath was made for man" (Mark 2:27). This cannot mean less than that the Sabbath was made for man's observance and for his benefit. God's glory and our good are always inseparably connected: whatever He has appointed us to heed and do in order for His honour, it is equally our wisdom and gain to comply with. If, then, the Sabbath was made for man's observance, it is self-evident that he is under Divine authority to submit thereto. Ere passing from this verse, let it also be pointed out that since the Sabbath was necessary and profitable for man in his first estate, when free from sin—remember that man was not exempt from labour in Eden, as the words "to dress it and to keep it" (Gen. 2:15) prove!—then how much more so now in order to recover him from his corrupt condition!

In the remainder of this chapter we shall devote our attention to the primitive observance of the Holy Sabbath, confining ourselves to its history in the earliest ages, namely, to the recognition thereof before its formal renewal in Exodus 20. It is frequently asserted that the Sabbath law originated at the time when Jehovah wrote the Ten Commandments on the tables of stone. But as we have shown, that is an error. The Sabbath was instituted before man fell. We would now inquire what evidence is there of men's keeping the Sabbath prior to Israel's reaching Sinai. Before answering this question, let it be pointed out that if there were none at all this would by no means convince us that the Sabbath was unknown before Exodus 20. An argument drawn from silence is always inconclusive. No mention is made of circumcision from the time of Joshua until the Babylonian captivity, yet how fallacious would be the inference that the rite had ceased to be practiced! Even though the Sabbath occupies so prominent a place in the institutions of Moses, yet it is never mentioned again till the days of Elijah (nearly 700 years later), and then only an incidental allusion is made to it (2 Kings 4:23).

There would be no need to wonder, then, in such particularly brief compendiums of history as are giver of antediluvian and Patriarchal times, if there should be a similar silence to those mentioned above. But is there a complete silence? Is there nothing in Scripture to indicate whether or not men kept the Sabbath before Israel reached Sinai? In seeking an answer we have to turn back to the book of Genesis and the first 18 chapters of Exodus, and ere we consult them it is well to remember their general character. No less than 25 centuries of human history are covered by those first 68 chapters of the Bible! Thus it is evident at once that the Holy Spirit has seen fit to give us little more than a bare outline of what transpired during the infancy of our race. Hence, we must not expect to find here anything more than a few references to the Sabbath, and these of the briefest nature. The same pertains to almost any other theme. There are unmistakable references to the Sabbath, but they are only incidental in character.

"And in the process of time (at the end of days) it came to pass, that Cain brought of the fruit of the ground an offering unto the LORD; and Abel, he also brought of the firstlings of his flock" (Gen. 4:3, 4). The very fact of Cain and Abel coming together, and this for the purpose of presenting an offering to the Lord, intimates that the time when they were thus engaged was a stated one, known to and recognized by them both—otherwise, what had induced the jealous Cain to unite with the pious Abel in this action? The bringing of offerings by Cain and Abel was the formal recognition of God: it was an act of devotion. Moreover, it is expressly stated that they worshipped God "at the end of days," the Divinely appointed season.

And when was that? Exactly what is signified by "the end of days"? Surely the unprejudiced reader who comes to the Scriptures in childlike simplicity, desiring to learn the mind of God, will form only one concept here. He will naturally say, Why, the end of days must be the end of the week, and that, of course, is the Sabbath.

But can we prove what has just been advanced? Yes, by an appeal to the context. If the first three chapters of Genesis be read through, it will be found they mention one "end" and one only, and that is in Genesis 2:3: "On the seventh day God ended His work which He had made." Now as Scripture ever interprets Scripture, as its terms are defined by the way in which they are used in other passages, and as the law of the context is whatever fixes the meaning of any given clause, so here in Genesis 4:3, the "end of days" can only mean the end of the working week—the Sabbath. Thus this passage teaches us four things. First, that previous to the days of Cain and Abel a Sabbath had been instituted. Second, that this Sabbath came at the end of a week of work. Third, that it was recognized and owned by the sons of Adam and Eve. Fourth, that it was set apart for sacred use, namely, the worship of God.

We next turn to, "and he called his son Noah, saying, This same shall comfort us concerning our work and toil of our hands, because of the ground which the LORD hath cursed" (Gen. 5:29). Here we are told why Lamech named his son "Noah." The very fact that the Holy Spirit has recorded this detail must be because some important truth is illustrated thereby. Names were not given in those early days at the idle caprice of the parents. They were pregnant with meaning, frequently given under Divine guidance, often memorializing some event of importance. Plainly was this the case in our present instance. Lamech belonged to the godly line, being the son of Methuselah (whose name was certainly given under Divine impulse), the grandson of Enoch. Lamech called his son Noah, which means rest, giving as his reason, "this same shall comfort us concerning our work and toil of our hands." In the light of Genesis 2:3, 4, is not this profoundly suggestive? Did not Lamech, in the name given his son, express his gratitude to the great Creator for providing a weekly Sabbath as a rest from "work" and "toil"? It was a pious heart looking forward to the Rest of which the weekly Sabbath was both the type and pledge.

"And it came to pass on the seventh day that the waters of the flood were upon the earth" (Gen. 7:10, margin). This verse records the beginning of the great Deluge and its terms are the more noteworthy because in the next verse we read, "In the six hundredth year of Noah's life, in the second month, in the seventeenth day of the month, the same day were all the fountains of the great deep broken up and the windows of Heaven were opened." Surely the Spirit had some good reason for giving us both of these time-marks. The second of them is obviously the historical reference: why, then, are we first told that the Flood began "on the seventh day"? Clearly because the reference here is a moral one, a word of explanation. It makes known to us one of the reasons, perhaps the chief one, why God visited the earth with such sore judgment. It conveys a solemn message to us: the flood began on the Sabbath Day! Is not the inference inescapable? Was it not an act of, what men term, poetic justice? Doubtless the antediluvians had flouted the Sabbath institution as they had every other Law of God. They had desecrated His Holy Day: therefore, when the Lord visited His wrath upon them it was on the Sabbath that the Flood commenced!

"And he stayed yet other seven days . . . and he stayed yet other seven days" (Gen. 8:10, 12). These references make it clear that way back in Noah's day the division of time into weeks was a recognized custom, for the repetition here makes it evident this was no casual or arbitrary act on his part. This fact has not received the attention it deserves. How was it, why was it, and when originated this division of time? We submit that this hebdomadal revolution of time furnishes another striking testimony to the primitive Sabbath. We quote now from the late B. H. Carroll, President of the S. W. Baptist Seminary: "I ask you to notice this strange historical fact, that for all other divisions of time we have a reason in the motions of the heavenly bodies. The revolution of the earth around the sun marks the division of time into years. The moon's revolution around the earth gives us the month. The day comes from the revolution of the earth upon its axis. But from what suggestion of nature do you get the division of time into weeks? It is a positive and arbitrary division. It is based on authority. The chronicles of the ages record its recognition. But how did it originate? Here in the oldest book, in the first account of man, you will find its origin and purpose. Noah twice recognized it in the ark, when he waited seven days each time to send out his dove. Jacob in the days of his courtship found it prevalent when he looked for satisfaction in the laughing eyes of Rachel, and the stern father said, "fulfil her week" (Gen. 29:27). Why a week? How did he get it? It was God's division of time.

Yes, it was God's division of time. Why should our week have seven rather than six or 10 days? and why have men everywhere adopted this measure? A primeval Sabbath explains it: it is the key to an otherwise insoluble enigma. Since there is no prominent natural phenomenon visible to every eye which can account for it, we are obliged to deduce some ancient institution coeval with our race, from which it spontaneously originated. That institution was the Sabbath, in which the Creator set apart one seventh of man's days for the worship of Himself. Thus did the Architect of the universe write His signature across time itself, and never shall it be erased.

In his masterly dissertations on the Sabbath, John Owen showed that no impartial and pious mind can entertain any doubt that there was a free observance of the Sacred Day by the Patriarchs: we give a very brief digest of his argument. The creation of the world was one of their principal articles of faith, as the Apostle asserts in Hebrews 11:3—then how vain to imagine they had utterly lost the tradition of the rest of God upon the finishing of His works. That the Patriarchs did observe the solemn worship of God in and with their families is clear from Genesis 18:19 and other passages, and for that some stated time was indispensably necessary; and what ground have we to suppose they were left without Divine direction in this important matter? The testimony which is given to them, that they walked with God and obtained a good report, the fact that they are said to have kept "the way of the Lord" and "His charge" (Gen. 26:5), all point to the same conclusion.

"And Abraham set seven ewe lambs of the flock by themselves" (Gen. 21:28). In this connection it is striking to note how that the ancients, universally, regarded the number seven as having a mystical significance. Seven times did Jacob bow before Esau in proof of his submission to him; seven years did he serve Laban for Rachel, and seven more for Leah. The number seven had, for some reason or other, obtained special favour in the families of Abraham, Isaac and Jacob. The same obtained also among other branches of the race of Shem. The history of Job, for example, who lived in the early times of the postdiluvian age, relates that when his friends came to comfort him they, "sat down with him upon the ground seven days and seven nights" (2:13)—and when (later) the Lord bade him offer sacrifice on their behalf, He said, "take unto you now seven bullocks and seven rams, and go to My servant Job," etc., (42:8). Balaam evidenced the same mystical reverence for this number (Num. 23:1). This writer is firmly convinced that the sacredness which from earliest times attached to the mystical "seven" has its roots in the primeval Sabbath.

There is yet another trace of the Sabbath in the early ages of the world to be found in Exodus: a most striking one it is, though it seems to have quite escaped the notice of those who have written on this subject. One reason for the deliverance of Israel from Egypt was that they might be free to keep the Sabbath and to offer those sacrifices and observe those ordinances which were connected with it. "

Thus saith the LORD God of Israel, Let My people go, that they may hold a feast unto Me in the wilderness" (5:1), "Let My people go, that they may serve Me" (9:1). Do not these words clearly imply that while sojourning in Egypt the Israelites had been prevented from observing their religious ordinances? Their merciless taskmasters had blotted out their Sabbath and made their life one ceaseless round of toil and misery. This is clearly confirmed by the words of Pharaoh to Moses and Aaron: "And the king of Egypt said unto them, Wherefore do ye, Moses and Aaron, let (hinder) the people from their works? get you unto your burdens. And Pharaoh said, Behold, the people of the land now are many, and ye make them (not "cease" but) REST from their burdens" (Exo. 5:4, 5). Evidently one of the first things the intrepid Moses did when he returned to Egypt was to insist that his brethren keep the Sabbath, and hence Pharaoh's objection.

3. ITS RENEWAL

In order to bridge the small gap between this and the last chapter, we must ponder a very striking passage in Exodus 16, from which we may learn some facts of deep importance concerning the existence and observance of the Holy Sabbath prior to Israel's reaching Sinai. That chapter records God's giving of the manna as Israel's daily food while they were in the wilderness. First, "Behold, I will rain bread from Heaven for you; and the people shall go out and gather a certain rate every day, that I may prove them, whether they will walk in My Law or no. And it shall come to pass, that on the sixth day they shall prepare that which they bring in; and it shall be twice as much as they gather daily" (vv. 4, 5). From these verses it is unmistakably clear that a Divine Law was in existence before the Ten Commandments were inscribed on the tables of stone, and from what follows it is equally evident that the observance of the Sabbath was part of this self-same Law: in no other way can these words of God to Moses be explained.

The Lord was about to give His people a daily supply of manna, and made it known to Moses that a double supply should be furnished them on the sixth day—to make up for none being given them on the seventh. In this respect Exodus 16 is parallel with Genesis 2:2, 3, inasmuch as once more we see the Creator condescending to be the Exemplar of His creatures: Jehovah manifested His regard for the Sabbath by withholding manna on that day. "We may here observe three miracles in honour of the Sabbath, and to secure it against desecration were wrought every week before the promulgation of the Law at Sinai. Double the quantity of manna fell on the sixth day. None fell on the Sabbath. The manna preserved for that day did not corrupt" (Robert Haldane).

Next we are told, "And it came to pass on the sixth day they gathered twice as much bread, two omers for one man: and all the rulers of the congregation came and told Moses" (v. 22). Now note very particularly the definite language of Moses in reply, "This is that which the LORD hath said, Tomorrow is the Rest of the Holy Sabbath unto the Lord" (v. 23). This is the first express mention of the "Sabbath" in the history of Israel, and the terms in which it is here introduced utterly precludes the absurd idea that the Sabbath was then, for the first time formally and legally instituted. No candid mind reading this chapter for the first time would ever conclude that here was a most important religious ordinance, quite unknown before, now given to the people. Rather is it not obvious to any careful reader that throughout the whole of this narrative two facts (unnamed) were in the mind of the writer, without regard to which the account is unintelligible: that a Divine Law was binding on the people (by which they were to be proved afresh), and that they had a sufficient knowledge thereof as to be expected to keep the Sabbath.

The words of Moses in verse 23 are brought in only incidentally, in answer to a question put to him by the elders: the substance of which is, the people have done quite right in gathering a double supply of manna on the sixth day. Moses was far from speaking in the style of one promulgating a new law, nor do we find him giving any detailed instructions as to the manner in which the seventh day was to be kept. The Wilderness of Sin was far from being the birthplace of this blessed ordinance: these scenes described in Exodus 16 obviously point us back to an earlier and primeval appointment. But ere passing on let us duly note that the words of Moses in verse 23 affirmed the three principal features of the Sabbath: first, it is designed for "rest"; second, it is "holy"—set apart from the six working days; third, it is to be kept "to the Lord": that is, it is a day for Divine worship and service.

"And it came to pass, that there went out some of the people on the seventh day for to gather, and they found none. And the Lord said unto Moses, How long refuse ye to keep My commandments and My laws?" (vv. 27, 28). Here we have illustrated the universal rebellion of the human heart. Here we have exemplified the common tendency to desecrate God's holy day. Even after the most explicit instructions to rest on the seventh day (v. 23), some of the people went out "for to gather." And mark God's response: "How long refuse ye to keep My commandments and My laws." This was not the first time that Israel had profaned the Sabbath: the words "how long" prove this.

They also confirm what we said above on verse 4: long before Sinai was reached, Israel had God's commandments and laws. Jehovah Himself says so, and the man who denies it, no matter what his standing or reputation, is guilty of the awful sin of making God a liar. "How long refuse ye" looks back to the wicked conduct of Israel while in Egypt.

Finally, observe how verse 29 supplies one more proof that Sabbath observance was no new thing at this time: "See, for that the LORD hath given you the Sabbath, therefore He giveth you on the sixth day the bread of two days; abide ye every man in his place, let no man go out of his place on the seventh day." Mark the careful distinction in the verbs used here: "the LORD hath given you the Sabbath, therefore He giveth you on the sixth day the bread of two days." What excuseless ignorance, then, is betrayed by those who affirm that the Sabbath was first instituted at Sinai. It is either ignorance or willful perversion of the Scriptures, and charity requires us to conclude that it must surely be the former.

We are now to consider the renewing or reinforcing of the Holy Sabbath at Sinai. "Remember the Sabbath Day to keep it holy. Six days shalt thou labour, and do all thy work. But the seventh day is the Sabbath of the LORD thy God: in it thou shalt not do any work, thou, nor thy son, nor thy daughter, thy manservant, nor thy maidservant, nor thy cattle, nor thy stranger that is within thy gates. For in six days the LORD made Heaven and earth, the sea, and all that in them is, and rested the seventh day, wherefore the LORD blessed the Sabbath Day and hallowed it" (Exo. 20:8-11). The Ten Commandments were uttered immediately by the voice of

God Himself in the hearing of all the people (Exo. 19), whereas all the other laws (whether ceremonial or judicial) were given through Moses. Those Ten Commandments, and they alone, were twice written by the finger of God on tables of stone, to denote their durability and permanence. The Ten Commandments were put inside the sacred ark itself, whereas the other laws (written in a book by Moses) were only placed in its side.

But if God in those ways emphasized the supreme momentousness of the Ten Words, giving them a place superior to all other laws, He also signalized in a peculiar way the outstanding importance and value of the Fourth Commandment. First, it is marked with a particular memento above the other commands: "remember"—partly because of our proneness to neglect, and partly because of its vast importance. Second, it is noticeable that the other nine are expressed simply, either negatively or positively, but this one both ways: "keep it holy . . . in it thou shalt not do any work" as if God put particular care to fence it on all sides. Third, its striking position in the Decalogue: it is put at the close of the first table and before the beginning of the second, to signify the observance of both tables depends radically upon our obedience to this particular precept.

It is indeed instructive to observe—O that we may have ears to hear—how the Lord God has fenced this particular commandment with more hedges than any of the other nine, to prevent our violation thereof and to render excuseless any trifling therewith. In addition to what has been pointed out above, we note, fourth, this commandment has more reasons to enforce it than has any of the others. God has therein condescended to give three cogent arguments to press the observance of this law upon us. The first is taken from His own example, which certainly it is both our glory and our duty to imitate in all things in which He has proposed Himself to be our pattern: God rested on the seventh day, and so must we. The second reason is taken from the bountiful portion of time which God has allowed us for the affairs of this life, namely, six-sevenths of our days, and

32

therefore it is but fitting and equitable that the seventh should be devoted to God. Third, from the dedication of the seventh day to God's immediate worship and service: "the Lord blessed the seventh day and hallowed it."

Let us observe that the character of those reasons wherewith God enforces the Fourth Commandment contain in them a most forcible argument to show that the Sabbath is perpetually binding. Negatively, we note there is nothing whatever in those reasons which suggest that the Sabbath ordinance was a ceremonial institution, or that it was to be regarded as being among those things which were typical of Christ to come in the flesh, which things were therefore to be abolished at His coming. Positively, there lies upon us today an obligation just as strong and binding as rested upon the Jews of old, for we equally with them are duty-bound to heed the example which the Creator set His creatures at the beginning. We are clearly required to own God as the Lord of our time by devoting one seventh thereof to His worship, and we certainly need the blessings attendant on a due observance of the Sabbath as much as ever did the Israelites in Old Testament times.

It is often asserted that Sabbath observance was made binding on the Hebrews only. But this is a most serious error. Not only is the Fourth Commandment of perpetual force, but it is universally binding: the arguments made above for the former, apply with equal force to the latter. The tribute which the Fourth Commandment demands for God is unquestionably due Him from all His creatures alike. This Commandment is "holy and just" (Rom. 7:12), and as the Apostle shows in that chapter, is also "good," for Gentiles as much so as for Jews. We could imagine some reason for saying that the Fifth Commandment has an exclusive Jewish cast, because the promise subjoined to it refers to long life "in the land." This it might be supposed was something spoken to the Jews alone. But such a supposition is immediately ruled out of court by Ephesians 6:1, 2— note "this IS (not "was") the first commandment with promise."

"The ground on which the obligation to keep the Sabbath is based in the Commandment is the most universal in its bearing that could possibly be conceived: 'Remember the Sabbath Day to keep it holy . . . for in six days the Lord made Heaven and earth.' There is manifestly nothing Jewish here, nothing connected with individual interests or even national history. The grand fact out of which the precept is made to grow is of equal signification to the whole world, and why should not the precept be the same? It seems, indeed, as if God, in the appointment of this law, had taken especial precautions against the attempts which He foresaw would be made to get rid of the institution, and that on this account He based its foundations first in the original framework and constitution of nature" (P. Fairbairn). What spiritual mind can doubt that this was what regulated Him who knew the end from the beginning.

How utterly futile are all these quibblings of men. How baseless their contentions. How strikingly were they anticipated and refuted by the Lord from the start. Why the very terms of the Fourth Commandment itself bring its obligation to bear upon the Gentiles! So far from obedience to this precept being limited to the Jews, it legislated also for "the stranger that is within thy gates"! Observe how godly Nehemiah enforced the observance of it upon the Gentiles as well as the Jew: "There dwelt men of Tyre also therein, which brought fish, and all manner of ware, and sold on the Sabbath unto the children of Judah and in Jerusalem. Then I contended with the nobles of Judah . . . I commanded that the gate should be shut and charged that they should not be opened till after the Sabbath" (Neh. 13:16-19). It was the observance of it and not the obligation of it which was peculiar to the Jews. It was placed in their custody for the good of all mankind.

The Fourth Commandment in the Decalogue was not the original institution of the Sabbath, but rather its formal renewal and reenforcement. As we have shown, the actual sanctification and appointment of the Sacred Day

34

of rest in worship takes us back to Eden itself, synchronizing with the very creation of man. It has also been shown that there are quite a number of unmistakable traces of the Sabbath being actually observed by God's people in the very earliest days of human history. But after the family of Jacob settled down in Egypt, they soon learned the ways of the heathen and, to a considerable extent at least, abandoned the instituted worship (Gen. 26:5) of Jehovah. Ezekiel 20:4-8 leaves us in no doubt that it was because of their idolatry the Lord employed the Egyptians in so severely chastising them.

"And they shall no more offer their sacrifices unto demons, after whom they have gone a-whoring" (Lev. 17:7). The reference here is to Israel's wickedness while sojourning in the land of Pharaoh: as Joshua 24:14 tells us, "Put away the gods which your fathers served on the other side of the flood (see vv. 2, 3) and in Egypt," and as Ezekiel 23:3 declares, "They committed whoredom in Egypt." It was pure grace which moved the Lord to deliver His wayward people from the house of bondage, and enter into a covenant with them. But grace ever reigns through righteousness, and never at the expense of the requirements of holiness. Accordingly Jehovah, in a most awe-inspiring manner, renewed His Law at Sinai, and intimated its lasting character by inscribing it on stones by His own finger; in the very center of which He placed the Sabbath statute. God has given us liberty to follow our lawful callings throughout the six working days, and therefore it is but little for us to devote the seventh to Him.

"Remember the Sabbath Day to keep it holy." "Remember": call to mind its original institution; cherish it in your affections; duly meet its just requirement, "The Sabbath": the sacred rest: its merciful freedom from temporal toil, its opportunities for obtaining deliverance from bondage of sin, its foreshadowment of the Eternal Rest awaiting those who now walk obediently to the Divine statutes. "To keep it holy": sever it from common use and consecrate the same to the service of God. It is no less a sin than

35

a sacrilegious stealing of that which is holy to purloin any part of that time which God has consecrated to Himself and to employ in it either sinful or secular activities. How the Sabbath is to be observed, what works are permissible and what are not, will be considered by us (D.V.) later.

4. ITS POLLUTION

The importance and value of the Sabbath is evidenced by the many, varied, and precious objects which, from the dawn of its institution, it was designed to accomplish. Under the Patriarchal dispensation it was a real and powerful witness for the existence of God, His creative power, His sovereignty over His creatures, and their responsibility to Him—truths which lie at the very foundation of all true religion. Under the Mosaic economy the Sabbath not only bore continued testimony to those truths, but also to the providential and moral government of God in the preservation and renewal of the Holy Day and His indisputable title to the worship of His people. It bore testimony to His gracious concern for their temporal and spiritual welfare—it taught them to look, through its hallowed use, for blessings on themselves and their nation—it pointed to a future period of richer blessing and purer worship. Under the Christian era, while all these fundamental truths are still inculcated by the Sabbath, it has become also a memorial of redeeming love, a witness for the establishment of the better covenant, a remembrance of Him who was delivered for our offenses and raised again for our justification.

It has often been pointed out that the Sabbath is not secured from man's pollution by any natural fences. The winter prevents much labour; obliging employers in many cases to reduce the tasks of their employees. Night is still more obstructive of toil, and consequently, still more conducive to needful repose. In the absence of light, the fields cannot be plowed, the crops harvested, nor homes built; and thus darkness serves to protect the couch of the heavy laden. But the Sabbath has no such bulwarks. It comes without any cosmic herald of its advent, and all nature fulfils its functions on that day as on any other day. The weather may be so inclement as to present no temptation to engage in outdoor sports; on the other hand, the day may be one of cloudless sunshine, alluring into the wide open spaces. Thus the Sabbath is like a vine when bereft of its hedges, which any boar out of the wood may waste, and any beast of the field devour. While the institution of the Sabbath is itself a fence to the general interests of religion and a Divine bulwark thrown up to repress the floods of ungodliness, yet the Sacred Day is not secured from profanation by any defenses furnished by the natural world. Thus we may perceive how admirably the Fourth Commandment serves as a trial of the attitude of the creature toward his Creator. There are few, if any, of the Divine ordinances that more definitely operate as a moral and religious test of the children of men than the one we are here considering. The conduct of men with reference to the Lord's Day most clearly discovers either their love or their hatred, their loyalty or their rooted enmity to Jehovah, their sovereign Lord. In proportion as nations, churches, or individuals increase in spirituality and morality, they venerate and improve this holy day; and to the degree in which they decline from the love of God and belief of His Truth, they despise and pollute it. The whole of human history forcibly illustrates that fact.

Allusion has been made by us to the natural obstacles which the seasons present to labour, and the protection they are designed to afford the labourer, yet these have been forced to yield to the pressure of greed and the merciless grind of commerce. During winter, at any rate in "civilized" (?) countries like our own, labour is never given a prolonged holiday, but instead its tasks are varied. And now the night (still more indispensable to our feeble frames) is disturbed and abridged, till it inadequately suffices for its gracious purpose. As the day comes to a close, artificial light is requisitioned, and in numberless instances the artisan is compelled to work "overtime"—and what compensation for the undermining of his health, and what is far worse, the degrading of his soul, is the extra wages he draws? How far the transportation of the workers and the noise of the "night shifts" interfere with the slumbers of other toilers, it is impossible to estimate—no wonder that institutions for nervous wrecks and mental cases are multiplying.

If, then, the protected seasons of nature have been ruthlessly invaded and trampled upon by graspers after gold, then much more is the unprotected Sabbath exposed to very special and imminent jeopardy. But the very fact that it is so exposed only serves to make more real the test it furnishes for the state of our hearts. Private gardens are railed off, and thus are secured from the carelessness and vandalism of the rank and file of the people; but those parks and downs which are open to the general public furnish a criterion to the manners and conscientiousness of those who use them, or abuse them—as the litter they leave behind bears witness. Thus it is with the Holy Sabbath. The righteous call it "a delight, the holy of the Lord, honourable," and they honour Him by not "doing their own ways, nor finding their own pleasure, nor speaking their own words" (Isa. 58:13). But the ungodly say, "When will the new moon be gone, that we may sell corn? and the Sabbath, that we may set forth wheat?" (Amos 8:5).

At no one point has the depravity of fallen men been more conspicuously, more blatantly, and more constantly displayed, than by their profanation of the Sabbath. From earliest times they have discovered their awful rebellion against their Creator and Governor by trampling upon His holy institution. As we have pointed out earlier, there is good reason to believe that one of the principal grievances which the Lord had against the antediluvians was their disregard for and desecration of this primitive ordinance. So, too, with the descendants of Jacob after they settled in Egypt—as the language used by Jehovah in Exodus 16:28 so plainly implies. For centuries past the Hebrews had despised His Law and dishonoured His Sabbaths; and for that very reason His anger waxed hot against them and they were made to suffer His sore judgments (Ezek. 20:8, etc.). And as we shall now see, there was little or no improvement in the later conduct of the Nation as a whole.

After the Lord had acted with such wondrous grace toward His refractory people, and by His mighty power delivered them from the house of bondage, one would have thought their hearts would have been so affected that their subsequent ways were amended. Moreover, the awe-inspiring display which Jehovah gave of His majesty on Sinai and the covenant which He there entered into with the Nation, ought surely to have resulted in a radical change of their behaviour. But alas, neither the goodness nor the severity of God makes any real and lasting impression upon men until they are born again. No matter what mercies they may be the recipients of, no matter how wondrously God deals in providence with them, and no matter how solemnly He makes known to them His sovereignty and holiness, they continue unchanged, unmoved, till they be renewed in their souls. Clear and awful proof of this was furnished by them in the Wilderness.

In order to obtain a complete picture of Israel's conduct in the Wilderness, not only must we attend diligently to the historical accounts furnished by the Pentateuch, but we must also search for the additional information supplied by the Prophets, for in many instances their retrospective statements supplement the former. Here, as everywhere, Scripture must be compared with Scripture. It is to Ezekiel that we are again indebted for fuller light on the point now before us. Reviewing the past, the Lord said through him, "I wrought for My name's sake, that it should not be polluted before the heathen, among whom they were, in whose sight I made Myself known unto them, in bringing them forth out of the land of Egypt. Wherefore I caused them to go forth out of the land of Egypt, and brought them into the wilderness. And I gave them My statutes, and showed them My judgments, which if a man do, he shall even live in them. Moreover, also I gave them my Sabbaths, to be a sign between Me and them, that they might know that I am the LORD that sanctify them" (20:9-12). And what was their response to such grace on His part?

Here is the sad answer to our question, "But the house of Israel rebelled against Me in the wilderness: they walked not in My statutes, and they despised My judgments, which if a man do, he shall even live in them; and My Sabbaths they greatly polluted: then I said, I would pour out My fury upon them in the wilderness, to consume them. But I wrought for My name's sake, that it should not be polluted before the heathen, in whose sight I brought them out. Yet also I lifted up My hand unto them in the wilderness, that I would not bring them into the land which I had given them, flowing with milk and honey, which is the glory of all lands. Because they despised My judgments, and walked not in My statutes, but polluted My Sabbaths" (Ezek. 20:13-16). What a tragic picture does that present to us of the generation of Israel which came out of Egypt! How it discovers to us the inveterate wickedness of the human heart. Unaffected by the Divine goodness, they now despised God's statutes and polluted His Sabbaths. And how heavily punished were they for their disobedience? They were excluded from the land of promise and condemned to die in the wilderness. Ah, my reader, God is not to be mocked with impugnity; and remember, this Divine judgment of Israel is recorded as a warning for us today.

And what effect did that fearful deprivation have upon their children? Did they profit from the warning? Did they turn from the evil ways of their fathers, which had so sorely displeased Jehovah? Surely, surely, with such a solemn judgment before their eyes, they would turn it to good account. Every opportunity to do so was then given to them: "Nevertheless Mine eye spared them from destroying them, neither did I make an end of them in the wilderness. But I said unto their children, in the wilderness, Walk ye not in the statutes of your fathers, neither observe their judgments, nor defile yourselves with their idols: I am the LORD your God: walk in My statutes, and keep My judgments, and do them; and hallow My Sabbaths; and they shall be a sign between Me and you, that ye may know that I am the LORD your God" (Ezek. 20:17-20).

Alas, the younger generation were no better than the old: no more amenable to Jehovah's exhortations, no more restrained by fear of His judgments. "Notwithstanding, the children rebelled against Me: they walked not in My statutes, neither kept My judgments, to do them, which if a man do, he shall even live in them; they polluted My Sabbaths: then I said, I would pour out My fury upon them, to accomplish My anger against them in the wilderness. Nevertheless, I withdrew Mine hand, and wrought for My name's sake, that it should not be polluted in the sight of the heathen, in whose sight I brought them forth. I lifted up Mine hand unto them also in the wilderness, that I would scatter them among the heathen, and disperse them through the countries; because they had not executed My judgments, but had despised My statutes, and had polluted My Sabbaths, and their eyes were after their fathers' idols" (vv. 21-24). It is to be duly noted that in each of these passages the Lord, while making the general complaint that Israel rebelled and walked not in His statutes, specifically singles out for mention the heinous crime that they had "polluted His Sabbaths," for that is something which He will by no means tolerate, and fearful indeed are His judgments upon those who are guilty of such an high offense.

Nor was there any improvement after Israel entered and was established in Canaan. To the people of Ezekiel's own day, the Lord complained, "Thou hast despised Mine holy things and, hast profaned My Sabbaths" (22:8). The order of those two things is solemn: it is because we despise the things of God that we pollute them. But still worse is what we read of in verse 26 of this chapter: "Her priests have violated My Law, and have profaned Mine holy things . . . And have hid their eyes from My Sabbaths." Not only was the general public guilty of this sin, but the ministers of God were offenders too. They turned a blind eye to the requirements of the Sacred Day, conniving at the joining in of its profanation. Those religious leaders esteemed not those who kept the Sabbath, and winked at those who did servile work therein.

So, too, we find the Lord saying through Jeremiah, "Hear ye the word of the LORD, ye kings of Judah, and all Judah, and all the inhabitants of

Jerusalem, that enter in by these gates: thus saith the LORD; Take heed to yourselves, and bear no burden on the Sabbath Day, nor bring it in by the gates of Jerusalem; neither carry forth a burden out of your houses on the Sabbath Day, neither do ye any work, but hallow ye the Sabbath Day, as I commanded your fathers" (17:20-22). Note this message was addressed first to the "kings of Judah," the heads of the Nation, for the heaviest weight of responsibility ever rests on those in the chief places of governmental power; and second, to the people at large. And what was Israel's response to this Divine call? This: "But they obeyed not, neither inclined their ear, but made their neck stiff, that they might not hear, nor receive instruction" (v. 23). Alas, what is man? The same in every age, under all circumstances: self-willed, defiant, refusing to be in subjection to his Maker; blind to his own interests, forsaking his own mercies, deaf to all reproof and admonition.

Patiently and faithfully did the Lord expostulate with His wayward people, setting before them the certain alternatives of their conduct: "And it shall come to pass, if ye diligently hearken unto Me saith the LORD, to bring in no burden through the gates of this city on the Sabbath Day, but hallow the Sabbath Day, to do no work therein; then shall there enter into the gates of this city kings and princes sitting upon the throne of David, riding in chariots and on horses, they, and their princes, the men of Judah, and the inhabitants of Jerusalem: and this city shall remain forever. And they shall come from the cities of Judah, and from the places about Jerusalem, and from the land of Benjamin, and from the plain, and from the mountains, and from the south, bringing burnt offerings and sacrifices, and meat offerings and incense, and bringing sacrifices of praise unto the house of the LORD" (vv. 24-26). What inducements were these to render loyal and loving allegiance to their King! The Lord is no Egyptian taskmaster. Not only is His yoke easy and His burden light, but He gives most liberal wages to those who serve Him. True is this for individuals and communities alike. Here is another Scripture which makes it abundantly clear that the chief thing on which national prosperity turns is its careful observance of the Sabbath.

If on the one hand Israel would not be moved to obedience by promises of rich reward, perhaps they might be deterred from disobedience by threats of terrible judgment. Accordingly, Jehovah concluded by saying, "But if ye will not hearken unto Me to hallow the Sabbath Day, and not to bear a burden, even entering in at the gates of Jerusalem on the Sabbath Day; then will I kindle a fire in the gates thereof, and it shall devour the palaces of Jerusalem, and it shall not be quenched" (v. 27). Alas, Israel was as indifferent to the latter as they had been to the former. How strictly God made good His threat appears from, "came Nebuzaradan, captain of the guard, a servant of the king of Babylon, unto Jerusalem: and he burnt the house of the LORD, and the king's house, and all the houses of Jerusalem, and every great man's house burnt he with fire" (2 Kings 25:8, 9). This was a national calamity in consequence of national pollution of the Sabbath. Following upon the destruction of the Temple and the raising of Jerusalem, the people were carried into Babylon. Seventy years later, God, in His mercy, opened a way of escape for the people from their captivity, and thousands of their descendants returned to Jerusalem. Had they at last learned their lesson?

Did they now hearken to the voice of God's rod and mend their ways? No, they were incorrigible. Hardly had they arrived back in the holy land than Nehemiah had to complain, "In those days saw I in Judah some treading winepresses on the Sabbath, and bringing in sheaves, and laden asses; as also wine, grapes, and figs, and all manner of burdens, which they brought into Jerusalem on the Sabbath Day: and I testified against them in the day wherein they sold victuals" (13:15). And then he added, "Did not your fathers thus, and did not our God bring all this evil upon us, and upon this city? Yet ye bring more wrath upon Israel by profaning the Sabbath" (v. 18).

Thus it was all through the long centuries of Israel's history. Nor has the conduct and career of Christendom been any better. While today it is far worse than for generations past. Here, in Great Britain, Sabbath desecration is now almost as rife as it is on the Continent, and only here and there is a feeble voice raised in protest. Sad to say the heads of the Nation often set a bad example by travelling on the Sabbath Day. The flood of Sunday newspapers which deluges the land, the irreligious rubbish which is being broadcast over the air, the increasing number of public places open for sport and entertainment, and the millions of people who turn the Holy Day into one of pleasure and "joyriding" is surely heaping up for us wrath against the Day of wrath unless we, as a people repent and reform.

5. ITS PERPETUATION

We now approach what is to us, upon whom the ends of the ages are come (1 Cor. 10:11), the most pertinent and important aspect of our subject. It is therefore necessary to proceed slowly and enter more into detail, especially as there is so much confusion and error at this point. In seeking to open up this branch of our theme, we feel that we cannot do better than follow more or less closely the lucid and helpful writings of P. Fairbairn thereon. We would like to quote him at length, but this would occupy too much space, so we content ourself by summarizing his able exposition thereof, intermingling and adding some remarks and conclusions of our own.

First, a Christian Sabbath was clearly anticipated by Old Testament prophecy: or to put it another way, the Prophets plainly intimated that the Holy Sabbath would be perpetuated throughout the Christian dispensation. Thus we have a natural bridge which connects the Old and New Testaments together. A wide field is here opened for investigation, but for the sake of brevity and clarity, we shall confine our attention to two predictions: the first one enunciating the basic general principle, the second furnishing more explicit details. We have discussed the former passage under the Covenant articles in our Studies in the Scriptures, but for the sake of our new readers, and particularly as it bears upon our present theme, we must again look at it.

Before turning to those ancient evangelic testimonies, it should be pointed out that a considerable portion of the prophetical writings pertains rather to the New, than to the Old Testament dispensation. They were designed to deliver the Jews from dwelling too exclusively in their thoughts on their present regime; on which they were ever prone to settle with a carnal and exclusive regard; and to direct the eye of faith forward to those better things which were to come, and which were to be disclosed in "the dispensation of the fullness of times" (Eph. 1:10). It was of those very things, the prophecies we are to consider, spoke. They were "the testimony of Jesus," witnessing beforehand of the work He was to do, the nature of that kingdom which He would establish, and the character of those blessings He should confer.

In proof of our contention that the Sabbath obtains for the Christian dispensation, we appeal first to, "Behold, the days come, saith the LORD, that I will make a new covenant with the (spiritual) house of Israel, and with the (spiritual) house of Judah: Not according to the covenant that I made with their fathers, in the day that I took them by the hand to bring them out of the land of Egypt; which My covenant they break, although I was a husband unto them, saith the LORD. But this shall be the covenant that I will make with the house of Israel: After those days, saith the LORD, I will put My Law in their inward parts, and write it in their hearts; and will be their God, and they shall be My people. And they shall teach no more every man his neighbour, and every man his brother, saying, Know the Lord: for they shall all know Me, from the least of them unto the greatest of them, saith the Lord: for I will forgive their iniquity, and I will remember their sins no more" (Jer. 31:31-34). That the new covenant here mentioned is that brought in by Christ is expressly affirmed in the eighth chapter of Hebrews, so that there can be no doubt of this being one of those prophecies which had immediate reference to the Gospel economy.

Now the leading characteristic of this New Covenant, as contradistinguished from that which was made with carnal Israel at Sinai, is that God's Law is now written on the hearts of His people, whereas it was formerly written on tables of stone: in this the Law is transmitted internally, in that, the Nation had it externally. Yet, let it be said emphatically, it is identically the same Law: the Moral Law, not the ceremonial, for so far from that being exalted into a higher place by Christ, it was in Him abolished, passing away like the shadow when the substance comes. Nor is the ceremonial law ever designated absolutely "the Law of God," and least of all could that be meant when the Law and the Covenant are viewed (as they are here) as in great measure identical. That which is pre-eminently called "the Law" in the Pentateuch and which formed exclusively the old covenant, was simply the Ten Commandments—those wholly and those alone.

It was the Ten Commandments, then, which the Spirit of Prophecy (through Jeremiah) foretold should one day, namely, in the Gospel dispensation—be inscribed by the finger of God upon the hearts of His people. By a miracle of grace being wrought in them, they would, after the inward man, delight in and serve God's Law (Rom. 7:22, 25). It could not be otherwise, for God has predestinated them to be conformed to the image of His Son (Rom. 8:29)—initially so now, fully so in Glory. If then the Head could say, "I delight to do Thy will, O My God: yea, Thy Law is within My heart" (Psa. 40:8), so in their measure can the members of His mystical Body say the same. Yet there is this great difference—for in all things He has the pre-eminence: Christ was born ("that Holy thing": Luke 1:35) with God's Law in His heart, whereas it is only written in ours at the new birth.

Now if the Ten Commandments as a whole are written upon the hearts of Christians it must be true of each individual part—the Fourth as well as any of the rest. That Commandment was most certainly included as an essential part of the Law or Covenant which was formerly written without and set before the Nation of Israel, but is now written within and infused with living power in the affections of the souls of God's people. And is not that very fact attested by Christian experience? How uniformly do they who are admitted into the privileges of the New Covenant love and delight in the Day of God! Nay, the more deeply anyone drinks into the spirit of the Gospel and experiences the grace of God writing the Law of holiness on the tablet of his heart, the more invariably does he count the Sabbath "the holy of the Lord and honourable."

So far from a renewed soul chafing at the restraints which the Day of Rest throws upon his conduct, and hankering after a larger freedom amid the pleasures and business of the world, he gladly hails its hallowed employments, and finds its weekly returns as so many "spring days" in his spiritual nature. He thinks and feels with the poet:

"Sweet day of rest! for thee I'd wait,
Emblem and earnest of a state
Where saints are fully blest!
For thee I'd look, for thee I'd sigh.
I'd count the days till thou art nigh
Sweet day of sacred rest!"

The second passage to which we appeal for proof of the Sabbath in this dispensation is, "Neither let the son of the stranger that hath joined himself to the LORD, speak, saying, The LORD hath utterly separated me from His people; neither let the eunuch say, Behold, I am a dry tree. For thus saith the LORD unto the eunuchs that keep My Sabbaths, and choose the things that please Me, and take hold of My covenant: Even unto them will I give in Mine house and within My walls a place and a name better than of sons and of daughters: I will give them an everlasting name, that shall not be cut off. Also the sons of the stranger, that join themselves to the LORD, to serve Him, and to love the name of the LORD, to be His servants, everyone that keepeth the Sabbath from polluting it, and taketh hold of My covenant; even them will I bring to My holy mountain, and make them joyful in My house of prayer; their burnt offerings and their sacrifices shall be accepted upon Mine altar: for Mine house shall be called a house of prayer for all people" (Isa. 56:3-7).

Now it should be unmistakably evident to all that the above prediction does and could not refer to Jewish but must relate to Gospel times. First, this is clear from the place it occupies in the chain of prophecy, and of which it is a part—i.e., beginning at 54:1 immediately after the atoning death of Christ in chapter 53. Second, it is directly connected with the revelation of "God's righteousness" and the "coming near of His salvation" (56:1), which can only be understood of Gospel times (see Rom. 1:16, 17), and is so regarded by all sound interpreters. Third, express mention is here made of the keeping of the Sabbath as a characteristic mark of godliness on the part of the "strangers" (Isa. 56:6) that is, the Gentiles who should join themselves to the Lord—"To the Lord," and not to the Nation of Israel!

It is also to be noted that the duty and blessedness of observing the Sabbath are spoken of in Isaiah 56:4 as belonging to the "eunuchs," who under the Mosaic dispensation were excluded from the congregation of the Lord, as also were the "strangers" as a body. Now the calling of the Gentiles and the removal of all outward, personal disabilities in God's sight, are emphatically marks of the New Testament Church; yet of such a Church it was definitely predicted that the observance of the Sabbath would form a distinctive characteristic. Finally, not only is the observance of the Sabbath three times repeated with singular emphasis, but it is coupled with laying hold of the Covenant, doing justice, and loving the name of the Lord—clearly importing that the Sabbath has its place with the most important and permanent appointments of God's kingdom.

Ere passing on, perhaps it will be well for us to anticipate an objection which some may be inclined to make against what has just been advanced. The dispensationalists, who are so fond of allocating to a Jewish "millennium" those prophecies which receive their fulfillment under this Christian economy, are likely to say Isaiah 56:3-7 cannot be understood as receiving its accomplishment in Gospel times, but must be regarded as describing conditions under a future and restored Judaism, because verse 7 says, "their burnt offerings and their sacrifices shall be accepted upon Mine altar." From this and other passages the grotesque conclusion is drawn that an era yet to come is to witness a revival of the ancient Levitical ritual—a thing which is not only without a vestige of New Testament support, but which is expressly refuted by the entire contents of the Hebrews' Epistle, the special design of which is to show that the Aaronic priesthood has been forever set aside, superseded by the more excellent priesthood of Christ after the order of Melchizedek.

Surely only those who are blinded by prejudice could fail to see that so far from Isaiah 56:7 containing anything in favour of a future restored Judaism, the whole passage in which that verse occurs makes dead against such a preposterous view. Why, if there be any one thing more than another which outstandingly characterized the exclusiveness of Judaism, it was that the priestly functions were rigidly confined to the family of Aaron. "Therefore thou (Aaron) and thy sons with thee shall keep your priest's office for everything of the altar, and within the veil; and ye shall serve: I have given your priest's office unto you as a service of gift: and the stranger that cometh nigh shall be put to death" (Num. 18:7 and cf. 3:10, 38). In passage after passage "death" is threatened the "stranger" (Gentile) who dared to approach that altar. So strict was Jehovah in the enforcement of this restrictive statute, that even when one of Israel's own kings dared to usurp sacerdotal functions by burning incense upon the altar, He smote him with leprosy (2 Chron. 26:16-20)!

What shall be thought, then, of those "renowned Bible teachers," who are supposed to have so much more light than the rank and file of ministers, when they display such ignorance of one of the most elementary principles of Judaism, and give forth such a carnal and absurd interpretation of the prophetic Scriptures? Why, to put it as charitably and mildly as possible, that they are unsafe guides in spiritual things, and that though they may be able to amuse the curious, they cannot edify those seeking a closer walk with God. This childish and slavish "literalism" is so far from honouring God, that it brings His Holy Word into disrepute among sober-minded people. Anyone who possesses spiritual discernment and who is at all acquainted with the New Testament, should at once perceive that the "burnt offerings" of Isaiah 56:7 are the same, as the "spiritual sacrifices" of 1 Peter 2:5, expressed in the terminology of the Old Covenant.

What a blessed picture does Isaiah 56 furnish of the distinctive and special blessings of Gospel times! New Covenant privileges are portrayed under the figures of Old Covenant institutions, yet such remarkable contrasts are drawn that there is no excuse for mistaking their purport. Both eunuchs and strangers were expressly excluded from the sacred precincts of Israel's tabernacle and temple, and to here affirm that the Lord would give them a "place in His house," is only the Old Testament way of saying that the "middle wall of partition" would be broken down. When in verse 6 it says, "the sons of the stranger that join themselves to the LORD, to serve Him," the same Hebrew word is used as signifies the service of the altar: in other words, it was a prophetic announcement that the redeemed from the Gentiles were made "a royal priesthood" (1 Peter 2:9) to offer no material and outward sacrifices, but spiritual and inward ones, the holy exercises of renewed hearts. The wild idea that it is "millennial" blessings which are here portrayed, is conclusively discountenanced by, "I will give them an everlasting name" (Isa. 56:5).

But to proceed: that the Sabbath should be continued throughout our own dispensation is just what might be expected, for the merciful nature and tendencies of the weekly Day of Rest is in perfect accord with the character and genius of Christianity. If a day of stated rest, on which all labour was forbidden as unlawful, and nothing permitted save what ministered to the life and well-being of the soul (with the exception only of works of necessity and mercy), was appointed by God for the good of His creatures under the Old Covenant, then certainly such a gracious provision is equally suited to the character and design of the New Covenant. If there be any feature of Christianity in its connection with human society, more prominent than another, it is the tenderness it breathes toward the poor and needy, and the beneficial influence it is fitted to exert on the conditions of those who require most of sympathy and kindness.

Christ Himself gave it as the leading characteristic of His work on earth that thereby the objects of deepest compassion were relieved, and that the poor had the Gospel preached unto them (Matt. 11:4, 5). There was in His heart an infinite tenderness and fellow-feeling for such, even in regard to temporal evils, which often excited the wonder of His immediate followers and rebuked their comparative indifference. And is not a weekly Sabbath, bringing a periodical release from the toils and burdens of life, permitting the most weary and oppressed a season of repose in the bosom of their families, and to attend to what they must otherwise neglect, namely, the higher interests of their being—is not such a Day an unspeakable boon to the great bulk of mankind? Has not the Sabbath been one of the most wise and benevolent gifts the Creator has bestowed upon His creatures, testifying His care both for their bodies and their spirits, by providing relaxation for the one and refreshment for the other?

Undoubtedly that is the real character of the Sabbath. And if Christianity has done anything to destroy the foundations on which such a blessed institution rests, it must surely in this particular, be strangely inconsistent with its general tendency and design. In its care for the poor and oppressed—it must then actually rank lower than Judaism, and be chargeable with removing one of the noblest bulwarks of the weak against the strong—of the labouring classes of society against the greed and grind of the monopolists. That the Gospel of the grace of God was intended to produce such an unfavourable effect, or can be made to do so otherwise than by some gross perversion of its meaning, will not readily be believed by any who know what the spirit of the Gospel is. The benevolent character of the Gospel, viewed in connection with the equally benevolent character of the Sabbath, amounts to a strong presumption that so far from subverting, the one must rather establish and support the other.

To continue, let the reader ponder carefully the following questions. Does a weekly return of a day, separated from ordinary employment and consecrated to the immediate service and worship of God, seem to run contrary to the evident scope and tendency of the Gospel, or rather to harmonize with it? Does it tend to promote or hinder the end which Christianity has avowedly in view? Is it relished or disrelished by those who have drunk most deeply into the spirit of the Gospel? And when it is allowed, more or less, from whatever cause, to fall into neglect, does the cause of Christ appear to gain or to lose in consequence? These are very important and most pertinent inquiries, and are not to be summarily dismissed by a prejudiced shrug or sneer.

It is neither fair nor fitting that such questions as the above should be disposed of by a general and unsupported objection that such an ordinance as the Sabbath is not in keeping with the spirit of the Gospel. We ask, in what respect is it not in accord? Does it beget a temper which the lessons of the Gospel are meant to subdue, or to check the growth of feelings which it calls us to cherish and manifest? If this were the case, it would go far to prove the unsoundness of any defense which might rather be raised for the Sabbath in this dispensation. But is it so? Wherein lies the supposed contrariety between the design and spirit of Christianity and the strict observance of a weekly Sabbath? To reply that the one promotes freedom while the other makes for bondage, is to confound liberty and license and is to mistake necessary restraint for serfdom.

It is almost universally acknowledged in Christendom that the Gospel, considered in its lowest aspect, is pre-eminently a scheme of benevolence, and that it looks with a kindly and friendly countenance on the condition of those who most stand in need of sympathy and care. But we ask, is not a weekly Sabbath, withdrawn from worldly employments, bringing to the very

54

busiest the liberty, at least, of relaxing their bodies and refreshing their spirits, one of the highest boons that can possibly be conferred on the poor? Certainly God Himself claimed it as one of His special acts of kindness toward Israel that He gave to them the privilege of knowing and keeping such a day. Are, then, the artisans of this materialistic, strenuous, and avaricious age, in less need of such a merciful furlough from their weekly toil? Then has the Gospel less concern for man's temporal well-being than had the Law?

But the Gospel has another, a higher, a far more prominent and peculiar characteristic than this, namely, its spiritual and holy tendency being pre-eminently designed to beget those who embrace it to a pure and heavenly life. In this respect it not only equals, but far surpasses Judaism. True it is, blessedly true, that the Gospel is not so much a revelation of law as of grace, nevertheless grace abounds only that believers may proceed to higher exercises of faith and godliness. Every doctrine it reveals, every privilege it confers, is avowedly designed to have its present fruit unto holiness, as well as its final end unto everlasting life. To be conformed unto the pure image of the Son of God, to have our affections set upon things above and not on things of the earth, to glorify God and not gratify self is the character at which the Gospel aims—which all its truths and ordinances are calculated to produce, and without which its great end is practically annulled. Hence the covetous, the lovers of pleasure, the earthly-minded, no less than the grossly impure, are expressly declared to be unfit for a place in the kingdom of God as now constituted.

Now as real Christianity is thus identified with a spiritual and heavenly character on the part of its professors, it is pertinent to ask, What relation has the institution of a weekly Sabbath, dedicated throughout to the worship and service of God, to such an object? Does it tend to promote, or rather to hinder and retard, this high design? The question is not whether men may not strictly adhere to the observance of a proper Sabbath, and yet resort to unhallowed practices on other days of the week, for hypocrisy can counterfeit a regard to this as to any other ordinance of God. No, it is, Is the Sabbath calculated to be a handmaid to the Gospel in producing the purifying effects at which it aims? Does a weekly day, divorced from all ordinary labour and devoted to religious exercises, tend to help forward true piety, or to mar and kill so desirable a fruit?

The question when thus directed to its proper object, admits of a speedy answer: not only is a day of holy rest greatly conducive to the end in view, but it is scarcely possible to conceive how, without such a day, the end could, among the bulk of mankind, be accomplished at all. Even under the Mosaic economy, when the standard of spirituality was confessedly lower than it ought to be now, the Sabbath was found necessary for the same purpose, and on this account especially did God set it to be "a sign between Him and His people throughout their generations, that they might know that He was the Lord that sanctified them." How much more, then, is it required now, when His people are called to live so much by the faith of what is spiritual and Divine, and to cultivate that elevated frame of mind and course of life which is indispensable to a close communion with God.

While it is true that the Gospel requires this heavenly mindedness and holy living to be common to every day of the week, and does not allow it to be confined only to one, yet take away the wholesome and hallowing influences of that one, constantly coming round with its sacred exercises, and what is likely to become of the rest? How soon will the bulwarks of piety give way, and the whole spirit and character of Christianity become secularized, if the Sabbath were practically abolished and every day of the week were alike devoted to worldly pastime or business. If the cause of Christ on earth is to prosper, and the great end of the Gospel to be promoted in the souls of men, then assuredly this day of holy rest to the Lord cannot be dispensed with, nor can it be too jealously guarded against the encroachments of worldly occupation, for it is through the sacred leisure and holy exercises of that day men are especially to familiarize themselves with the things of God.

Another way of ascertaining the relation which the Sabbath holds to practical Christianity is to inquire how they who have drunk most deeply into the spirit of the Gospel usually feel toward such a day. If we might entertain any doubt as to the proper connection between a Sabbath and the great ends of the dispensation of grace, we ought surely to have that doubt removed if we find the general pulse of the saints beating, as it were, in unison on the subject. We would seldom fail to gather aright the bearing of any particular measure on the constitution of a country, if we heard one and the same sentiment expressed regarding it by those who were most conversant about and imbued with the spirit of that constitution. So with the Sabbath. Can any such testimony be produced in its favour? Yes—in every generation of this era, the most pious have espoused and promoted its observance, and that not only in one country, but in every land where the Gospel obtains a footing. Pages might be filled with testimonies from one and another, but we will content ourselves with one only, who lived in the palmy days of Puritanism.

"For my part, I must not only say, but plead whilst I live in this world, and leave this testimony to the present and future ages, that if ever I have seen anything in the ways and worship of God, wherein the power of godliness hath been expressed: anything that hath represented the holiness of the Gospel, and the Author of it; anything that hath looked like it prelude to the everlasting Sabbath and rest with God, which we all through grace to come unto, it hath been there and with them where and amongst whom the Lord's Day hath been had in highest esteem, and a strict observation of it attended unto, as an ordinance of our Lord Jesus Christ. The remembrance of their ministry, their walking and conversation, their faith and love, who in this nation have most zealously pleaded for, and have been in their persons, families, and churches, the most rigid observers of this day, will be precious with them that fear the Lord, whilst the sun and moon endure" (John Owen).

We bring these arguments to a close by pointing out that it adds much to the force and conclusiveness of all that has been advanced above for the necessity of a Sabbath to the life and prosperity of Christianity. Whenever the observance of such a day falls into practical neglect, the consequence to the cause of Christ are most disastrous. Ministers of the Gospel and teachers and guardians of youth have often proclaimed the melancholy result of what they have witnessed in many lands that neglected or ill-spent Sabbaths infallibly result in their declining spirituality and decreasing morality. Chaplains of prisons have in like manner borne witness that the vast majority of offenders brought under their notice have been notorious Sabbath-breakers, and that many of them acknowledge their downward course began with neglecting its holy duties and privileges.

Thus far have we sought to show that the presumption in favour of the Sabbath being perpetuated during this Christian era amounts virtually to a demonstration. We now proceed to prove this presumption grows into certainty when we contemplate the personal conduct of the Lord Jesus Christ in connection with it, and ponder some of His declarations. Take first the former: "And He came to Nazareth, where He had been brought up; and, as His custom was, He went into the synagogue on the Sabbath Day" (Luke 4:16). Thus it is clear that the Saviour honoured this Divine institution. During the quiet years which preceded His public ministry, He had regularly attended the synagogue's services on that day specially set apart for sacred solemnities. It is striking to note that this statement occurs not in Matthew (the most Jewish of the Synoptists), but in Luke, where He is portrayed as the Son of man.

At the beginning of His public ministry, one of Christ's first announcements was, "Think not that I am come to destroy the Law, or the Prophets: I am not come to destroy, but to fulfil" (Matt. 5:17). Here the Lord asserted in most unequivocal language, that His mis- sion in this world was not designed in any respect to abolish or relax, but to verify and confirm what had previously been declared by God. The Redeemer accomplished what was required by the Law and the Prophets, first, by personally fulfilling in Himself that righteousness which they demanded; and second, by imposing the same upon His people as the measure of that obedience to which through His grace they were to be ever growing. To have ignored the demands of the Law or the Prophets in either of those respects, would manifestly have been to destroy and not to fulfil them.

Now the force of Christ's solemn assertion in Matthew 5:17 and its pertinence to our present inquiry is at once apparent if we pause to ask this specific question: Was the ordinance of the Sabbath equally recognized and enforced in the Law and the Prophets? Surely the question answers itself. In that solemn and comprehensive revelation of Law which was promulgated from Mount Sinai and which in Scripture is usually denominated "the Law," it had a definite, an honourable place, occupying the very center of the Ten Commandments. So, too, in the Prophets: not only when they spoke of Jewish, but also when they referred to Gentile times, there is (as we have shown) a testimony both explicit and authoritative in favour of the Sabbath. Thus, when Christ declared He came to fulfil the Law and the Prophets, He can only be fairly understood to mean that He definitely adopted the testimony they delivered concerning the day of Sacred Rest.

"And He said unto them, The Sabbath was made for man, and not man for the Sabbath: Therefore the Son of man is Lord also of the Sabbath" (Mark 2:27, 28). The Sabbath was designed for man's blessing. It was given because he needed it, both in his body and in his soul. It was appointed that he might be man in the highest sense of the word—something better than a beast of burden, something nobler than a cash register. Observe the force of, "Therefore the Son of man is Lord also of the Sabbath":

59

because the Sabbath is made not merely for Israel, but for man, and because in becoming incarnate the Son of God touched all humanity, as "Son of man" He is "Lord also of the Sabbath." And mark well His relation thereto: He is not the Destroyer of the Sabbath, but its "Lord"; not the Repealer of it, but its Sovereign.

There are a number of passages in the Gospels (like Matt. 12:1, 2, 10) which record the criticisms that the Saviour met with from His enemies regarding His conduct on the Sabbath, and it is most instructive and important to note the different answers He gave in self-vindication. That which is of chief moment for us to observe is that His utterances on these occasions made it unmistakably clear that both works of real necessity and works of mercy on the Sacred Day are permissible and lawful. Thus we discover that the words, "in it thou shalt not do any work" (Exo. 20:10) are not to be understood absolutely, but are to be interpreted in the light of these modifications of Christ. All Sabbath labour which is not imperative for the well-being of man and beast is Divinely forbidden, but whatever be essential for their true good is sanctioned by the Lord's own example.

Though Christ ignored all the rabbinical regulations which had been superimposed upon the Divine Law, He never did one thing or uttered one word which to the slightest degree undermined or relaxed the requirements of the Fourth Commandment. There is evidence that the Sabbath law had been encumbered and perverted by Jewish interpretations and traditions. They permitted a man to fill a trough with water for beasts to come and drink, but forbade him carrying water to them. According to one school it was not allowable to minister unto the sick on the Sabbath. Consequently we find our Lord going to considerable pains to expound the Fourth Commandment, and rescue it from these accretions. It was not that Christ modified the exactions of the Divine Law or granted man an indulgence for secularizing the Sacred Day, but that He freed it from the arbitrary injunctions of the Jewish teachers.

In what has just been pointed out, we discover another proof for the continuance of the Sabbath in this dispensation. If the Sabbath had been on the brink of being repealed, why should Christ have been so careful to explain its requirements, and make clear that works of mercy and of necessity were allowable on that day? Read carefully the various vindications which He gave them when attacked on that point, and where is there the slightest hint that He was about to abrogate the Sabbath? So far from it, His defenses, one and all, were simply to the effect that He was delivering it from the errors of the Pharisees, and thereby He settled a point which would afterwards be of great service to His Church. "Suppose you saw a man taking pains to restore a defaced inscription on a pillar, to remove from it the rubbish which had been heaped around its base, and to tear away the ivy that surrounded its summit, would you not infer it was his intention that its inscription should remain for the information of future ages? Such was the conduct of our Lord in reference to the Sabbath Law" ("The Sabbath Not a Mere Judaical appointment" by Andrew Thomsom).

"But pray ye that your flight be not in the winter, neither on the Sabbath Day" (Matt. 24:20). These words were uttered by Christ at the close of His public ministry. "The earliest possible period to which this direction can refer, is the siege of Jerusalem—a period at least 40 years after the ascension of Christ, that is, after the full establishment of the Gospel dispensation, and after 'the Gospel of the kingdom had been preached in all the world for a witness unto all nations' (v. 14 and cf. Col. 1:6). At such an advanced period in the Gospel age, and in a season, too, of unparalleled distress, the disciples were, by the direction of their Lord, to make it a matter of special prayer that they might not need to take their flight on the Sabbath Day . . . . It is impossible to entertain due respect to Christ as an infallible teacher, without admitting it to be His clear intention in this passage that the weekly Sabbath should continue after the Gospel dispensation was fully set up" (F. Fairbairn, from which much in this article is taken almost verbatim).

6. ITS CHRISTIANIZATION

That the Judaical Sabbath, as such, has been abolished, we unhesitatingly affirm; but to conclude from this that there is now no "Sabbath" in the strict and proper sense of that term, we emphatically deny. Serious errors have been committed at either extreme. On the one hand there has been an insignificant company who have vigorously contended that God has given no command for any change to be made in the weekly Day of Rest, and therefore that we, in this dispensation, are required to observe the seventh day. On the other hand, another class has insisted that the "Sabbath" has been completely abolished, though they allow that it is the privilege of Christians (any law requiring the same, they deny) to honour Christ in a special manner on the first day of the week. The Truth lies between these two extremes: the Sabbath remains, though it has undergone some noticeable changes in its Christianization.

A thorough inquiry into the precise differences between the Judaical Sabbath and the Christian Sabbath (deeply important as such an inquiry is)—differences as to its significance, its penal sanction, its day of observance, etc.—would require a full exposition of the Siniatic covenant; but as we recently went into that subject at length in our Studies, it is not necessary for us to traverse the same ground again. But a brief summary of its salient and distinctive features seems unavoidable. Originally, the Sabbath was "made for man" (Mark 2:27); it being required of him naturally, the light and law of nature suggesting that some time be set apart and dedicated to God for the observance of his solemn worship in the world. Man in his creation, with respect to the ends of God therein, was constituted under a covenant: the law of his obedience being attended by promise and threat, reward and punishment.

During the interval which elapsed between the Fall of Adam and the Lord's deliverance of Israel from Egypt, the nations had completely apostatised from God, and had been given up by Him to a spirit of blindness (Rom.

1:21-28). The dealings of God with the Hebrews marked a fresh and distinctive departure in the Divine ways with mankind. At Sinai the descendants of Jacob were taken into special covenant relationship with Jehovah. As the Sabbath had been originally annexed to the covenant between God and man (Adam, and the race in him), the renovation of the covenant (at Sinai) necessarily required an especial renewal of the Sabbath, and the change of the covenant as to the nature of it, necessarily introduced a change of the Sabbath. In what respects, we shall endeavour to point out.

When God erected His Church in the wilderness (Acts 7:38), renewing the knowledge of Himself and of man's duty toward Him, in the posterity of Abraham, He gave unto them afresh the precepts of the Law and the Covenant of Works, for the rule of their obedience, reducing the same to Ten Commandments written on tables of stone. As thus delivered by Him, it was the same for the substance of it with the law of our creation or the original rule of our covenant obedience unto God. Yet as thus inscribed, there was an innovation in it, both as to its form and the principle of obligation. In form it was now made objective and external; and the immediate obligation unto its observance was prefaced by motives peculiar to their state and condition (Exo. 20:2). Later, its observance was continually pressed upon them by reasons taken from their peculiar relation to God, with His love and benefits unto them. It was now no more a moral command only, equally regarding all mankind, but had a temporary regard given to it, which was afterwards to be abolished.

The Law was renewed as an ingredient in that economy under which God placed His Church at Sinai, though He did not bring His people under the Covenant of Works in all the rigour of it—relief being found, for those betaking themselves to it, in the promise of grace in Christ. Nevertheless, there was begotten in the minds of the people such a sense of the demands of the Law and their obedience thereto, that it "gendereth to bondage" (Gal. 4:24). Annexed to the Law was the promise of, "Do this, and live"; and the threat, "cursed is everyone that continueth not in all things which are written in the Law to do them." Consequently, the Covenant form given to the Law at Sinai rendered the obedience of the people to it in a great measure servile. The death sentence was pronounced upon those who desecrated the Sabbath (Exo. 35:2, 3).

The Moral Law, to which was attached many statutes of both a civic and ceremonial nature, was made the rule of the government of Israel, as a holy nation under the dominion of God Himself as their King. Thus the whole Decalogue as given at Sinai had a political use, that is, it was made the principal instrument of the polity or government of the Nation as peculiarly under the rule of God. Their polity, as to the kind of it, was a theocracy, over which God in a special manner presided as their Governor, and this was peculiar to that people. Hence the Sabbath amongst them came to have an absolute necessity accompanying it, of an outward carnal ordinance, under pain of death if they neglected the same.

Again—the Sabbath was made a part of their law for religious worship in their temporal Church state, in which and whereby the whole dispensation of the covenant which Israel was under, was directed to other ends. Thus it had the nature of a shadow, representing good things to come, whereby the people were to be relieved from the rigour and curse of the whole law as a Covenant. Hence, new commands were given for the observance of the Sabbath, new motives advanced, new ends and uses formulated, so as to accommodate it to the dispensation of the Covenant then in force, but which was afterwards to be removed and taken away, and with it the Sabbath itself so far as it had relation thereto. Therefore we have no hesitation in subscribing to the following words of Owen:

"All these things in the law of the Sabbath are Mosaic: namely, the obligation that arose to its observance, from the promulgation of the Law unto that people at Sinai; the limitation of the day to the seventh or last of the week, which was necessary to that administration of the Covenant which God then made use of, and had a respect to a previous institution; the manner of its observance, suited to that servile and bondage frame of mind, which the giving of the law on Mount Sinai did generate in them, as being designed of God so to do; the engrafting of it into the system and series of religious worship then in force, by the double sacrifice annexed to it; with the various uses in, and accommodation it had to the rule of government in the commonwealth of Israel; in all which respects it is abolished, taken away."

If, then, noticeable changes were made in connection with the Sabbath when God took the people of Israel into covenant relationship with Himself, need we wonder that other changes were made when the Siniatic covenant and constitution were abolished? In order to distinguish the Christian Sabbath from what had obtained for 15 centuries, was it not expedient, might we say, essential, that under the era of the new Covenant, it should be observed on a new and different day? But alas, the perversity of men has led not a few of them to argue from that very change of the day from the last to the first of the week, that the Sabbath itself is completely done away with under the Christian dispensation. They insist that an entirely new institution has displaced it, an institution which consists in a certain pre-eminence of the first day.

Once again we avail ourselves freely of the writings of P. Fairbairn, and point out, first, even if we could assign no adequate reason for the seventh day being dropped and the first substituted in its place, a mere change of that kind would certainly not outweigh, with any serious-minded believer, the arguments we have produced in support of a Sabbath reaching from the creation of the world to the destruction of Jerusalem. This is a chain which links together Moses and Christ, the Patriarchal, Levitical, and Christian times. We should certainly be the less disposed to set aside the large amount of evidence, and to view the change in question as in itself conclusive against the existence of a proper Sabbath, when we know that the first day, on being appropriated to acts of worship, received the name of "the Lord's Day" (Rev. 1:10). Why called emphatically His, but to intimate that He now claimed the same propriety in it that he had hitherto done in the seventh?

If the first day, as a day—that is, as a whole, and not some particular portion of it—is the Lord's, in a sense in which other days of the week are not, how can it possibly be so, except in being set apart for employments and services peculiar to itself, and more immediately connected with His own glory? Was not this very feature the distinctive characteristic of the seventh day: that it was God's day, because specially separated by Him for sacred purposes? And does not this very character appear plainly in the appellation, "the Lord's Day," as transferring to the first day of the week that which had, essentially, marked the seventh day from Adam until Christ?

The principal feature which had distinguished the Sabbath from the very first, as designed for all classes and generations of men, is that a seventh portion of our time should be specially devoted to the worship of God, rather than the precise day of the week being the thing on which attention was to be fixed. It is the remembrance of a seventh day, as distinguished from the other six constantly going before and coming after it, which formed the substance of the Fourth Commandment, and that the seventh day was to be regarded as the last, rather than the first day of the week, appears only in what is assigned to the original ground of the appointment. We have no reason, but rather the contrary, to think that the Lord intended it to be always and solely connected with His own procedure in the work of creation.

At the giving of manna in the wilderness, when the Sabbath was restored after a period of oblivion, caused by the hard bondage of Egypt, the seventh day was counted from the time of God's beginning to bestow the manna. And instead of bidding them to keep it as a mere memorial of creation, He more frequently enforced it on their regard as a sign of the Covenant which He had with them, and a memorial of His goodness in delivering them from the land of bondage. After all this, is it not preposterous to suppose that the mere change of the day from the last to the first of the week, so as more distinctly to connect it with another and better Covenant and render it the fit- ting memorial of a higher and more glorious work, should utterly destroy its obligation or alter its character?

Again—let it be duly considered that the change was not made capriciously but for weighty and important reasons connected with the new work and covenant of God as distinguished both from that to which it stood immediately opposed in Judaism, and from that to which more remotely, but still more essentially, it stood opposed in creation. The observance of the last day of the week, as peculiarly set apart for God's service, though belonging like circumcision to an earlier state of things, had yet come, in great measure, to be connected with the Covenant made at Sinai. It was appointed to be a sign of that Covenant, and the reason for the day as a memorial of creation ceasing in course of time to be maintained among the Gentiles, the observance of it came ultimately to be regarded as a public testimony on the part of the Israelites of their adherence to the Covenant made with their fathers.

The need for a change of day in connection with the Sabbath under Christianity should now be the more apparent. The worship of God on the seventh day had been so blended with and merged into Judaism, that it could not serve as a proper sign and testimony to the world of the faith of the Gospel, and therefore without such a change as was actually made, one important end of this Divine institution and ordinance must otherwise have been lost. For the same reason that God abolished circumcision as the outward mark of His covenant people, He set aside the Judaical Sabbath as such; and for the same reason that He appointed baptism as the distinctive uniform of the Christian (Gal. 3:27) has He signalized the first day of the week as the Christian Sabbath.

But if we go beyond Sinai right back to the Divine work of creation, a yet stronger reason will be found for this change in the Day of Rest. As a memorial of that work, the Sabbath cannot be now what it originally was, for sin has entered with its destroying power, and laid creation, as it were, in ruins. The once beautiful and glorious inheritance is now given up a prey to the spoiler; and a memorial of it, while it tells us indeed of God's first designs of goodness toward His creatures, tells us at the same time how those designs have been opposed, and nature's life and glory have been brought down within the gulf of death. We need then, for our peace and welfare, another work and covenant of God to repair the ruin of the first, and lay the foundation of a higher—even an imperishable glory.

A grander and more blessed production than the making of this material world has been achieved, even the bringing forth of a new creation, which cannot be marred by sin or Satan. The work of redemption immeasurably transcends in importance and value the work of the first creation, and hence it is most fitting that it should be signalized by a change in the Day of Rest to commemorate the rest of the Saviour from all His arduous and costly labours in the putting away of the sins of His people and His bringing in an everlasting righteousness for them. The transcendent work of Christ is therefore memorialized in the Sabbath by transferring it from the last to the first day of the week, for it was on that day the Redeemer rose triumphant from the grave as the Head of the new creation, the firstfruits of them that sleep, the prototype and pledge of a glorified humanity.

By the very act of His glorious exodus from the tomb, the Lord Jesus begets all who believe on His name unto an inheritance incorruptible, undefiled, and that fadeth not away (1 Peter 1:3, 4). How appropriate, how delightful, then, the change made in connection with the Holy Day! Instead of seeking to take occasion from that change to impair or destroy the

Sabbath, it should endear to us that blessed institution all the more. For it tells now, not so much of a paradise that has been lost, as of a better paradise that has been won; not so much of a covenant broken and a heritage spoiled, as of a covenant forever ratified by the blood of Christ and a kingdom that cannot be moved. If the corruptible work and covenant of nature had by Divine appointment its Sabbatical sign and memorial, must not this higher work and covenant much rather have it?

"If we refuse now to enter into the fellowship of Christ's rest by hallowing the day which He has set apart in His Church for spiritual rest and blessing, what is it in effect but to cut ourselves off from the hope of His redemption and declare our light esteem of His finished work? We conclude, therefore, that it is now, as it ever has been, the will of God that one whole day in seven should be kept holy to Himself; that since the resurrection of Christ, this has been Divinely appointed to be the first day of the week; and that this change, while it could do nothing to weaken the obligation of a proper Sabbath, was both necessary to make the observance of a Sabbath conducive to some of the ends for which it was appointed, and also gives to it the character which cannot fail greatly to enhance and endear its sacredness to every child of God" (P. Fairbairn, from whom much in the second part of this article is taken verbatim).

We have thus far, in our remarks upon the Christianization of the Sabbath, confined our attention mainly to two things. First, in pointing out that the many arguments advanced for the perpetuation of the Sabbath in this dispensation cannot possibly be rendered invalid by the mere fact of a change in the Day of Rest—that it most certainly does not follow from the first day of the week now being the one specially hallowed for Divine worship, a proper Sabbath as such no longer obtains. Second, we sought to show that a change of economy required a change in the day of Sabbath observance: if the New Covenant was to stand out with clear distinctness from the Old, then a new Day of Rest best accorded with and testified to the establishment of the same.

We are now to dwell more particularly on the fact that the first day of the week is the one ordained of God for the Christian Sabbath. We know that these pages are read by people of varied shades of thought, some of them having been brought up under quite different teaching from what others have received, and as we desire (under God) to help one and all, we often feel obliged to take up an aspect of a subject which will not appeal to the majority, yea which may seem to them quite needless. Some of our readers have been influenced by "Seventh Day Adventism," and we must confess that in our wide reading we have come across very little indeed which was calculated to solve their difficulties; and therefore we deem it well to enter carefully and with some detail into this point.

The old creation comprised in it the law of obedience of man unto God, this being implanted in his moral nature, which gave inclination unto the observance of it. The law of creation had a covenant inseparably annexed to it, as had also the Siniatic constitution. The immediate end of those covenants was to bring men by due obedience unto the rest of God, and as a pledge thereof and also a means of attaining it, the Day of Rest was instituted. All these things therefore must have a place also in the New Covenant belonging unto the new creation, the immediate end of which is our entrance into the rest of God, as the Apostle proves at length in Hebrews 4. But therein we are not absolutely to enter into God's rest as a Creator and Rewarder, but to God in Christ as Redeemer, the foundation of which is the work of God in the new creation, and the complete satisfaction or complacency which He finds in Christ's atonement.

Thus it should be apparent that the particular day of the week on which the Sabbath is to be observed, resolves itself into what Covenant we walk under before God. If the Siniatic covenant has been annulled, then of necessity the Day of Rest has been changed. On the other hand, to insist that the Sabbath as given to the Jews is not abolished requires us to perpetuate the whole system of Mosaic ordinances which stood on the same bottom with it. That this is not simply an inference or dogmatic assertion of ours, that it is actually a Scriptural proposition is clear from the whole argument of Hebrews 7-10. "For the priesthood being changed, there is made of necessity a change also of the law" (Heb. 7:12). "The covenant being changed, the rest which was the end of it being changed, and the way of entering into God's rest being changed, a change of the day of rest must of necessity thereon ensue" (John Owen). With these introductory remarks we now proceed to offer further proofs for the first day of the week being the Christian Sabbath.

First, it was plainly adumbrated in Old Testament times. This change in the weekly Day of Rest from the last to the first day of the week, that is, from the seventh to the eighth, as everything pertaining to the Christian era, was intimated under various types and shadows. The work of creation was finished in six days, and on the seventh God rested from His work, which completed a week, or the first series of time. The eighth day, then, was the first of a new series, and on that day Christ rose as the Head of the new creation. The eighth day is accordingly signalized in the Old Testament, pointing in a manner the most express to the day when Christ entered into His rest, and when in commemoration thereof His people are to rest.

Circumcision was to be administered unto children on the eighth day (Gen. 17:12). On the eighth day, but not before, animals were accepted in sacrifice (Lev. 22:27). On the eighth day the consecration of Aaron as high priest, and his sons, after various ceremonies, was completed (Lev. 9:1). On the eighth day was the cleansing from issues, emblematic also of sin (Lev. 15:29). On the eighth day atonement was made for the Nazarite who was defiled (Num. 6:10). When the sheaf of the firstfruits was brought to the priest, it was to be accepted on the eighth day (Lev. 23:11)—a distinctive type of the resurrection of Christ. The eighth day was sanctified

71

at the dedication of the Temple (2 Chron. 7:9), and in its sanctification at the time of Hezekiah (2 Chron. 29:17).

Now, can any spiritual mind suppose for a moment that this repeated use of the eighth day, in connection with the most solemn services of God's ancient people and in a manner so conspicuous, was without a special purpose? Did not the wisdom of God single out that day for some very important end? intimating thereby an antitypical new beginning? The eighth day corresponds with the first day of the week, on which according to all those appointments, Christ was received as the Firstborn from the dead, His sacrifice accepted, and on which, as the great High Priest He was "consecrated for evermore," having made atonement for His people, by which they are cleansed from all sin. That purpose of God is fully developed in the New Testament, where He who is Lord of the Sabbath, without in the slightest degree changing the obligation to observe a seventh day, appropriated to Himself the first instead of the last day of the week.

Second, this change is clearly intimated by what is recorded of the first day in the New Testament. The alteration in the day of Sabbath rest and worship was emphasized by Christ's personal visitations to His assembled disciples on the first of the week. After His appearing to the travelers to Emmaus, the Saviour was seen no more until His mysterious and blessed manifestation in the upper room. "Then the same day at evening, being the first of the week, when the doors were shut where the disciples were assembled for fear of the Jews, came Jesus and stood in the midst, and saith unto them, Peace be unto you" (John 20:19). What is the Holy Spirit's object here in mentioning the particular day of the week? Was it not to inform us that this was now a particular day? Jews would understand at once what was signified by the notice that a religious "assembly" occurred on the seventh day, and Christians are to equally understand what is denoted by such an allusion to the first day.

The next detail to be noticed in the above passage is, "the doors were shut where the disciples were assembled for fear of the Jews." What is indicated by those words? Let it be remembered that the Lord had already "opened their understandings that they might understand the Scriptures" (Luke 24:45), which must mean that, in a measure at least, they now knew the types had given place to the reality. We also know that, "He through the Holy Spirit had given commandments unto the Apostles whom He had chosen, to whom also He showed Himself alive after His passion by many infallible proofs" (Acts 1:2, 3). What other conclusion, then, can be drawn, but that the disciples now observed the Sabbath on the first day of the week, and that they therefore took the precaution of fastening the doors because they knew how incensed the Jews would be for their departure from the ancient observance of the Sabbath on the seventh day?

Thomas was absent on the above occasion, and when he learned of its marvels, expressed strong unbelief. Throughout that week the Lord Jesus did not reappear. But when the disciples assembled again on the first day of the next week, Thomas being present with them, He once more stood in their midst and said, "Peace be unto you" (John 20:26). Is there nothing marked by that interval of time? His other interviews with them are not thus dated! Surely the fact that Christ was not seen by His disciples for a whole week, and that He then appeared to them again on the first day when they met for special worship, clearly signifies His definite sanction of this as the appointed day of meeting with His disciples? And is not this most expressly confirmed by the Holy Spirit's advent at Pentecost? Most assuredly the Spirit's descent on the first day of the week crowned this ordinance and ratified the newly instituted Christian Sabbath.

Third, the first day of the week was celebrated by the early Church. That this was how the Apostles understood the matter appears from their custom, for they assembled together for the breaking of bread and the preaching of the Word "on the first day of the week" (Acts 20:7). Are we not compelled to conclude that what the Apostles did, and what the churches did under their supervision, must have been done in accord with the revealed will of their Divine Master? But, it will be objected, If God requires the Sabbath to be duly observed on the first day of the week during this Christian dispensation, why has He not given a definite command through His Apostles to that effect in the Epistles? To this question we make three replies.

In the first place, it savors strongly of impiety: a taking it upon ourselves to say how God is to make known His pleasure to us—He has other ways of declaring His will besides through express precepts. In the second place, such a question loses sight altogether of the situation in which many of the early Christians found themselves—a situation very different from that which generally obtains today. In the first generation of the Christian era it was quite impossible for the Sabbath to be kept with the same sacred strictness with which the Jewish Sabbath had been observed. So long as the Christian Church was confined to the boundaries of Palestine, and its members were made up of Jewish believers and proselytes, as it was for some time, it was required of all the converts to continue in an exact observance of the Jewish Sabbath in compliance with the law of the land. They did, in addition, observe the Lord's Day, so far as that was possible privately; but they had it not in their power to render the first day one of holy rest for all their fellows.

When the Christian Church enlarged her borders and converts from the Gentiles added thereto, the Christian Sabbath had to encounter most formidable obstacles and was met by almost constant opposition. Let it also be carefully borne in mind that many of the early Gentile converts were the slaves of heathen masters, and it will at once appear how impossible it was for the Church to secure anything approaching Sabbath observance, so far as that implies the setting apart of the first day from all secular interests and the devoting of it solely unto Divine worship. It was therefore most merciful on God's part to lay not upon them a burden which they could not have borne. Nevertheless there is clear evidence that those early Christians devoted at least a part of the first day to special worship so far as their distressed and persecuted state rendered possible.

But in the third place, we ask, Is it true that no Divine command for the sanctification of the first day is to be found in the Epistles? And we reply, No, it is not. "Now concerning the collection for the saints, as I have given order to the churches of Galatia, even so do ye. Upon the first day of the week let everyone of you lay by him in store, as God hath prospered him, that there be no gatherings when I come" (1 Cor. 16:1, 2). "I have given order," is certainly the language of authority, and cannot be regarded as anything less than an apostolic command. It is to be duly noted that Paul "gave order" concerning not only the principle of systematic Christian giving (for the relief of indigent saints), but also stipulated the time when such collections were to be made, that being appointed for "the first day of the week." Nor was such a regulation peculiar to the church at Corinth, as is intimated by his, "so I teach everywhere in every church" (4:17), "so ordain I in all churches" (7:17). Moreover, he expressly tells us, "the things that I write unto you are the commandments of the Lord" (1 Cor. 14:37).

"In view of this important verse, we may remark: there is here clear proof that the first day of the week was observed by the church at Corinth as holy time. If it were not, there can have been no propriety in selecting that day in preference to any other in which to make the collection. It was the day which was set apart to the duties of religion, and therefore an appropriate day for the exercise of charity and the bestowment of alms. There can have been no reason why this day should have been designated except that it was a day set apart to religion, and therefore deemed a proper day for the exercise of benevolence towards others. This order extended also to the churches in Galatia, proving also that the first day of the week was observed by them, and was regarded as a day proper

75

for the exercise of charity towards the poor and afflicted. And if the first day of the week was observed, by apostolic authority in those churches, it is morally certain that it was observed by others. This consideration, therefore, demonstrates that it was the custom to observe this day, and that it was observed by the authority of the early founders of Christianity" (A. Barnes).

It is abundantly clear, then, from this passage that the first day of the week was by Divine authority appointed for Divine worship—for this "collection" was an act of Christian fellowship. Ere passing on, it should be pointed out that the Greek which is here rendered "the first (day) of the week" is the very same expression that is employed by the four Evangelists in connection with the resurrection of Christ (Matt. 28:1; Mark 16:1; Luke 24:1; John 10:1), also in John 20:19 when He appeared to the disciples in the upper room. The word used is "Sabbaton," which means both "week" and "Sabbaths." Literally, then, it reads, "the first of the Sabbaths," the Holy Spirit using this particular term to denote the beginning of a new series. Thus we need not have the slightest hesitation in speaking of "The Christian Sabbath."

The Christian Sabbath was most strikingly honoured by Christ Himself in His glorious appearing on the isle of Patmos and the prophetic revelation which He there made to His servant John. In narrating the wondrous visions which he there received, the Apostle describes the time when they were given to him as, "on the Lord's Day" (Rev. 1:10). Now all the days of the week are the Lord's, but that one of them should be singled out and thus designated to distinguish it from the others, shows that this day is His in a peculiar sense, as specially devoted to His honour. It is called "the Lord's Day" for precisely the same reason that the holy feast is called "the Lord's Supper" (1 Cor. 11:20)—the one as a memorial of His death, the other of His resurrection. This particular designation supplies further proof that He is "Lord of the Sabbath" (Mark 2:28).

A number of testimonies are still extant that the Christians in the first three centuries observed the Sabbath on the first day of the week. "On the day which is called Sunday, all, whether dwelling in the towns or in the villages, hold meetings, and the memoirs of the Apostles and the writings of the Prophets are read, as much as the time will permit; then the reader closing, the president in a speech exhorts and incites to an imitation of those excellent examples; then we all rise and pour forth united prayers" (Justin Martyr, in his Apology: A.D. 150). Another witness of the same era is Eusebius, "All things whatever that it was duty to do on the Sabbath, these we have transferred to the Lord's Day, as more appropriately belonging to it, because it has a precedence, and is first in rank, and more honourable than the Jewish Sabbath. It is delivered to us that we should meet together on this day" (Comments on Psalm 92).

From the beginning God determined that the ruination of the old creation should be followed by the producing of a new creation, with a new law of that creation, a new covenant, and a new Sabbath rest, unto His own glory by Jesus Christ. The renovation of all things by the Mediator was Divinely foretold (Acts 3:21): it was to be a "time of reformation" (Heb. 9:10). From the Epistles we learn that this renovation of all things has been accomplished by Christ: "old things are passed away," etc. (2 Cor. 5:17)— the old covenant, the old order of worship, the Judaical Sabbath. "That in the dispensation of the fullness of times He might gather together in one all things in Christ, which are in Heaven and which are on earth; in Him" (Eph. 1:10): only those things pertaining to the Mosaic economy remain which are useful to our living unto God, and they abide not on their old foundation, but on a new disposition of them in Christ: cf., 1 Corinthians 9:21.

Thus it is with the Holy Sabbath: it remains, yet it has undergone a decided renovation. As the incarnation of God's Son affected the chronology of the world (for all civilized time is, by common consent, dated from the year of

His birth!), so His death and resurrection terminated the old covenant and ratified the new, and this necessarily resulted in a change of the weekly day of rest. We have already pointed out that the first day of the week as now being the one Divinely appointed for Sabbath observance was, first, adumbrated in the Old Testament types, where "the eighth day" is so conspicuous. Second, that it was clearly intimated by what is recorded in the New Testament: the first day being that of our Lord's resurrection and the day of meeting with His disciples. Third, that it was so celebrated by the early Church: Acts 20:7; 1 Corinthians 16:2.

We are now to consider, fourth, that this change was conclusively demonstrated in Hebrews 4. We will first call attention to the fact itself as there stated, and then endeavour to indicate and elucidate the course of the Apostle's argument in that chapter. In Hebrews 4:8 it is expressly affirmed, "for if Jesus had given them rest, then would he not afterward have spoken of another day." What this other "day" is, may be unequivocally ascertained from the context: it is the Holy Sabbath—"God did rest the seventh day from all His work" (v. 4). So, too, immediately after mentioning "another day" (i.e. another or different one from the "seventh") the Apostle went on to say, "There remaineth therefore a rest to the people of God" (v. 9). In proof of this and also to identify this "another day" he declared, "For He (not "they," but "He," which is Christ) that is entered into His rest, He also hath ceased from His own works, as God did from His" (v. 10).

What has just been pointed out is quite simple and easy to understand, but in order to grasp the force of the Apostle's argument we need to gird up the loins of our minds and attend very closely to his chain of reasoning. First, we must observe that here in chapter 4 he is continuing what he had said in chapter 3. There he gave an exhortation unto faith, obedience, and perseverance (3:1-6), and this he enforced by a quotation from Psalm 95, which contained a pointed exhortation and a solemn warning taken from the case of those who fell under Divine wrath because they were guilty of the sin contrary to the duties of faith, obedience, and perseverance (3:7-11). This he at once follows by making application of the warning unto the Hebrews, and by expounding certain expressions in this quotation which he had made from the Psalmist (3:12-18).

Because the words of Psalm 95 contain not only a warning applicable to New Testament saints, and more especially because those words also had interwoven in them a prophecy (note "promise" in Heb. 4:1) concerning the rest of God in Christ by the Gospel and our duty thereon, Paul proceeded to enlarge upon and confirm his exhortation in 3:12, 13, still using the language of Psalm 95 for that end. First, he propounds the duty which he aimed to press on the Hebrews (4:1, 2). Second, he established the foundation of his exhortation, by showing that the "rest" mentioned by David was still future when he wrote Psalm 95 (Heb. 4:3). Third, he enters into a careful discussion of and differentiates between the various "rests" of God (vv. 4-10). Fourth, he concludes by returning to and repeating his original exhortation (v. 11).

Let it be clearly grasped at this stage that the Apostle's design in Hebrews 4:4-11 was to confirm what he had laid down in verses 1-3, which we paraphrase thus: There is under the Gospel a promise of entering into the rest of God left or remaining unto believers, and they do enter into that rest by mixing the promise of it with faith. It was the more necessary to press this upon the Hebrews: that notwithstanding their ancient and present enjoyment of the land of Canaan, yet their fathers fell short of entering into God's rest because of their unbelief, and that now they (their children) were under a new trial or test, a new rest being proposed unto them in the promise. This he proves by a testimony out of Psalm 95, whereof he had previously treated in Hebrews 3.

Now the application of Psalm 95 to the case of the Hebrews was liable to a serious objection: the "rest" mentioned there by David seemed to be one long since past. If that were the case, then these Hebrews could have no new or fresh concern in it, and therefore could be in no danger of coming short of it. It was to remove such an objection, and to confirm what he had previously advanced, that the Apostle occupied himself in what follows, and this he does by a direct appeal to Psalm 95, showing from the proper signification of its words, from the time when it was written, and from the persons there addressed, that no other "rest" was there intended than what was here being proposed by him unto them, namely, the rest of God and His people in the Gospel.

The general argument insisted upon by the Apostle to support his design and establish his purpose, consists in an enumeration of all the various "rests" of God and His people mentioned in the Old Testament. From the consideration of them all, he proves that no other rest could be intended by the language of David in Psalm 95 than the rest of the Gospel, whereinto all who believe do now enter. This he arrives at, most logically, by a process of elimination. First, the rest "promised" (Heb. 4:1) in Psalm 95 was neither the rest of God from the works of creation, nor the Sabbath rest which ensued thereon (Heb. 4:4-6). Second, nor was it the rest of Canaan, which Joshua brought the people into (Heb. 4:7, 8). No, it was a spiritual rest which remained or subsisted for believers to enjoy now (vv. 8-10). We are now prepared to enter into detail.

In verse 3, three things are laid down. First, an assertion, which comprises the whole intendment of the Apostle in this passage: "For we which have believed do enter into rest." Second, a proof of that assertion from the words of the Psalmist: "As He said, As I have sworn in My wrath, if they shall enter into My rest," or as the Psalm reads, "They should not enter into My rest" (95:11). Third, an elliptical entrance into a full confirmation of his assertion and the due application of his proof produced unto what he had designed: "although the works were finished from the foundation of the world." Now that "rest" which believers enter through faith in Christ (cf.

John 16:33) is first and primarily the spiritual rest of God, and is not to be restricted unto the eternal rest in Heaven, though that will be the fruition of it. God rests in Christ (Isa. 42:1) and in His people (Zeph. 3:17).

"As I have sworn in My wrath, If they shall enter into My rest" (Heb. 4:3), or "that they should not enter into My rest." How did those words contain a confirmation of what has been affirmed in the preceding clause? Two ways. First, by an axiom of logic. It is a well-known rule that unto immediate contraries contrary attributes may be certainly assigned, so that he who affirms the one at the same time denies the other, and he who denies that one affirms the other. For instance, if I say it is "day," I also affirm it is not "night." If, then, those who believed not entered not into God's rest, then it logically follows that those who believe do enter into it. Second, theologically: according to the analogy of faith—every threat also includes a promise, and every promise has also the nature of a threat in it.

"Although the works were finished from the foundation of the world" (v. 3). In those words the Apostle began his answer to an anticipated objection against what he had asserted of the Gospel rest. Now all "rest" presupposes labour, consequently each several "rest" of God must have some work preceding it. So it was, first, with His rest in Genesis 2:2 that was preceded by the six days of creation. This the Apostle at once refers to in verse 4, "For He spake in a certain place of the seventh day on this wise, And God did rest the seventh day from all His works." Now as Owen so convincingly pointed out, God's rest here is not spoken of absolutely, with respect to Himself only, but rather with reference to an appointed rest that ensued thereon for His creatures to rest in with Him, for this is the Apostle's scope all through this passage. Hence he refers us back to the whole passage from which he quotes (Gen. 2:2, 3): and there we learn that God not only rested on the seventh day, but "blessed" it for the rest of man. Thus he first treats of the Sabbath in relation to the state of man under the law of nature.

"And in this place again, If they shall enter into My rest" (Heb. 4:5). The "in this" has reference to Psalm 95, which he is here expounding and applying to the case of the Hebrews. The word "again" emphasizes the fact that the Apostle is now alluding to the second "rest" of God and the proposal He made unto His People of their entering into it. At the finish of His work, God rested the seventh day and blessed it for a day of rest unto His creatures. And "again," on another occasion, He spoke of "My rest." What that "other occasion" was, Psalm 95 tells us: it was when Israel was in the Wilderness (Psa. 95:8). God had finished another series of miraculous works when He brought His people out of Egypt and conducted them through the Red Sea. Then He took them into covenant relationship with Himself (at Sinai), renewed the Law, and set before them the rest of Canaan. That a spiritual rest was then proposed unto Israel is clear from the Apostle's changing the Psalmist's, "they should not enter into My rest" (95:11) to, "If they shall enter"—the exclusion of some definitely implied the entrance of others into God's rest if they complied with His terms.

At the risk of being wearisome, but for the benefit of those desiring to really understand this passage, we will here summarize the force of the Apostle's reasoning so far as we have yet gone. God's rest was tendered unto and entered into by some (viz., believers) from the foundation of the world. It must therefore be another rest which the Psalmist (so long after) spoke of, and which the descendants of Abraham were afresh invited to enter into, as later in his discussion the Apostle more clearly proves. And they who deny any Sabbath rest from the beginning remove all foundation for Paul's discourse: had there been no rest from the foundation of the world what need for him to prove that the "rest" mentioned in Psalm 95 was not the original one, if there had been none such? The very object of the Apostle in again referring to Psalm 95 was to show that the "rest" mentioned by David was not that which was appointed from the beginning of the world, but a much later one.

What that second and later "rest" was, we have defined in the last paragraph but one, as the rest of Canaan—not merely external relief from their wilderness wandering, but an entrance into the spiritual rest of God. Ere proceeding further we give proof of this, for we will take nothing for granted. There was a rest of God under the Mosaic economy. The prayer about it was, "Arise, O LORD, into Thy rest, Thou and the ark of Thy strength" (Psa. 132:8)—the ark being the symbol and pledge of God's presence and rest. This "rest" of God followed upon the completion of His mighty works in bringing Israel into Canaan. After the establishment of His worship therein, He said of it, "This is My rest forever: here will I dwell" (Psa. 132:14)! God having entered into His rest in like manner as formerly (upon the finishing of His glorious work), two things ensued thereon. First, the people were invited and encouraged to enter into the rest of God. This the Apostle treats of in Hebrews 3 and 4: their entrance into that rest being conditioned upon their faith and obedience. Although some of them came short of it, because of their unbelief, yet others entered into it under the leadership of Joshua. Second, this rest, both of God and of His people, was expressed by appointing a day of rest which was a token and pledge of God's present rest in His instituted worship, and was designed as a means in the solemn observance of that worship to further their entrance into His rest eternally. Hence the seventh day was to Israel a special sign that He was their God and they His people.

While it is true that the Day appointed in connection with this second rest of God was the same as the first one, viz., the seventh, yet it was now established upon new considerations and unto new ends. The time for the change of the day of rest was not yet come, for the work of God in bringing Israel into covenant-relationship with Himself, conducting them into Canaan, and instituting His worship among them, was but preparatory to yet another work and rest. The Covenant of Works, to which the original Sabbath was annexed, being not yet abolished (but only modified), therefore the Day of rest was not then changed.

Now to proceed. The Apostle goes on to show that Psalm 95 prophetically intimated that there was yet to be a third rest of God— which His people were to enter into—an especial rest under the Messiah, which he here proposed unto the Hebrews and exhorted them to enter into (Heb. 4:11). In this third state there was to be a particular condition of rest, distinct from and superior to each of those which had gone before. To the constitution thereof, three things were required: some signal work of God completed, whereon He entered into His rest. Second, a spiritual rest ensuing therefrom, for them that believe to enter into. Third, a new day of rest to express this rest of God, and to be a pledge of our entering therein. These things we now further inquire into.

"Seeing therefore it remaineth that some must enter therein, and they to whom it was first preached entered not in because of unbelief" (v. 6). Here the Apostle draws a conclusion which is incisive, but observe carefully it is based on the principle that a promise is included in every conditional threat, for unless the word of the Psalmist, "they should not enter into My rest" may also be (deductively) understood as, "if they shall enter," that is, they shall providing they meet the conditions, there would be no force whatever in saying, "that some must enter." They who entered not in because of unbelief or "disobedience" were the adult Israelites who came out of Egypt. The rest of Canaan which they missed was typical of the present rest of believers in Christ.

"Again, He limiteth a certain day, saying in David, Today, after so long a time; as it is said, Today if ye will hear His voice, harden not your hearts" (v. 7). In this verse the Apostle confirms what he had just affirmed about a new rest and a new Day of Rest remaining for the people of God to enter into, and which rest he proposes unto them. After the institution of the Sabbath rest at the beginning, and after the proposal of the rest of Canaan to Israel in the Wilderness, God, in addition ("Again"), limited or designed and determined another particular rest and "day," which was neither of the former, namely, that of the Gospel. It is to be carefully noted that in this verse the Apostle expressly changes his terms: God had "limited" or "defined" not only a "certain" or "particular" rest, but a DAY, because, it was Paul's design to show that God had determined not only another (a third) "rest," but also another "day" as a pledge of this new rest.

The force of his argument in verse 7 is taken from the time when this "day" was limited or determined. Had those words of David (in Psa. 95) been uttered by Moses just before Israel entered the typical rest of Canaan, they might have been thought to pertain thereunto and to have contained in them an exhortation unto Israel as that season. But instead, it was "after so long a time," namely, 500 years after Moses, that God gave this message through the Psalmist. Consequently it must have related and referred to some other "rest" than Canaan, and some other "day" than the Jewish Sabbath. Therefore, there is still a promise remaining of entering into this (third) rest of God, unto which we must take heed that we come not short of it by unbelief and disobedience.

"For if Jesus [Joshua] had given them rest, then would He not afterward have spoken of another day" (v. 8). In this verse the Apostle removes a possible objection and gives further confirmation of his argument, by a particular application of it unto the point before him. That which he still insists upon is, his principal assertion from the words of David, namely, the rest prepared and proposed in the Gospel unto believers. To this the Hebrews might object: Although the people who came out of Egypt entered not into the promised rest of God, yet the next generation did so under Joshua—why then propose this rest unto us, and warn against our danger of missing it? This objection is conclusively set aside by showing that God in David proposed "another day" of rest unto Israel centuries after Joshua, and as no new Sabbath was appointed in David's time, his words must be understood prophetically. Hence there was a rest proposed unto the Hebrews (and so us) and "another day" to memorialize it.

"There remaineth therefore a rest [keeping of a Sabbath] unto the people of God" (v. 9). The Apostle here shows, in a brief summary, what had been conclusively established in his whole disquisition: three things indubitably followed. First, that a Divine and spiritual rest remains for the people of God to enter into and enjoy with Him. Second, that a Sabbath Day to memorialize it, and be a means of entering into that rest, abides under the Gospel. Third, that it must of necessity be "another day," a different one from that which obtained under the old covenant. It is to be duly noted that the Apostle did not say "there awaiteth" or "there is yet to be a Sabbath keeping," but "there remaineth." The reference is not to something future, but what is present. This word is used in the same sense when applied negatively to the system of sacrifices: "There remaineth no more sacrifice for sins" (Heb. 10:26). How striking that this occurs in Hebrews! The Levitical priesthood has been set aside, the temple is no more, Judaism is abolished: but a Sabbath remains!

We wish to call special attention to the fact that in verse 9 Paul again deliberately changed his terms. The word for "rest" here in verse 9 is an entirely different one from that used in verses 1, 3, 5, 8, 10. It is "Sabbatismos" which speaks for itself: the R.V. has, "There remaineth therefore a Sabbath rest for the people of God." It was a word coined by the Apostle to express the whole sense of that with which he was treating: that is, to denote both the rest itself and the appointment of "another day" as a token of it—it signifies our rest in God and the Day which is the pledge of it. And this Sabbatismos remaineth—the word "remaineth" signifies to be left after others have been withdrawn (as the primitive and Judaical Sabbaths have), to continue unchanged, as the Christian Sabbath will unto the end of the world. Here, then, is a plain, positive, unequivocal declaration by the Spirit of God: "there remaineth therefore a Sabbath keeping." Nothing could be simpler, nothing less ambiguous, for this is addressed to the "holy brethren, partakers of the heavenly calling" (3:1). Hence, we solemnly and emphatically declare that the man who says there is no Christian Sabbath takes direct issue with the New Testament Scriptures.

In our discussion upon the Christianization of the Sabbath we are seeking to establish (from Scripture) two things. First, that there is a Sabbath appointed by God for this dispensation—a Christian Sabbath for His people to keep holy and enjoy. Second, that this Christian Sabbath is to be observed upon "another day" of the week than the one celebrated throughout the Old Testament era. The one passage in the New Testament which above all others most conclusively proves both of these points is Hebrews 4:8-10, and therefore are we seeking to give a careful exposition of these verses and their setting.

Hebrews 4:9 expressly declares, "There remaineth therefore a rest [keeping of a Sabbath] to the people of God." Nothing could be simpler, nothing less ambiguous than that verse. The striking thing is that it occurs in the very Epistle whose theme is the superiority of Christianity over Judaism—a theme developed by showing the superiority of Christ (the Center and Life of Christianity) over angels, Adam, Moses, Joshua, Aaron, and the whole Levitical economy. It is an Epistle addressed to "holy brethren partakers of the heavenly calling" (3:1). Therefore it cannot be denied that Hebrews 4:9 is referring directly to the Christian Sabbath. Hence, we solemnly and emphatically declare again that the man who says that there is no Christian Sabbath takes direct issue with the New Testament Scriptures.

"There remaineth therefore a rest [keeping of a Sabbath] to the people of God" (Heb. 4:9). In this, and the following verse, the Apostle evidences the perfect analogy between the several rests of God and His people discoursed of in this chapter. First, at the beginning there was the creative work of God and His resting therefrom, which made way for a rest for His creatures in Himself and His worship by the contemplation of the works He had made. A day was specially assigned for that purpose—that was the primitive Sabbatismos. Second, there was a great work of God in bringing Israel out of Egypt and the establishing of His people in Canaan, which made way for their entering into His rest and worship, a Sabbath Day being appointed to express both the one and the other—this was the Mosaic Sabbatismos.

So now, under the Gospel, there is a Sabbath comprised of all these. As we shall see there was another and greater work of God, and a rest of His own ensued thereon. On that work is founded the promise of rest spiritual and eternal to those who do believe, and the determination of a new day expressive of the one and the other. This is the Christian Sabbatismos. That the redemptive work of Christ has not only secured this spiritual rest to His people, but has also necessitated and resulted in a new Sabbath to celebrate it appears from two things in the Apostle's discourse. First, by his referring to our Gospel rest by the name of DAY (v. 8). Second, from his coining of this term "Sabbatismos" to express both our spiritual rest and the Sabbath-keeping which memorializes the same.

"For He that is entered into His rest, He also hath ceased from His own works as God did from His" (v. 10). Plain and simple as these words are, yet they have been grievously wrested by most of the commentators. They are generally regarded as referring to believers entering into the rest of God, through their believing of the Gospel. But there are two considerations which expose the error of this view. First, the verse does not read, "they who enter into His rest," but "He that is entered into." Second, if the reference was to believers, what are the "works" from which they cease? Their sins, say some; their legalistic efforts to win God's approval, say others; their sorrows and sufferings, from which they shall rest in Heaven, say yet others. But how could they be said to rest from any such works, "AS God from His" own? It is utterly impossible to satisfactorily answer such a question. No, the verse speaks not of believers, but of Christ.

"For He that is entered into His rest, He also hath ceased from His own works, as God did from His." Here the Apostle concludes his argument by declaring that the "rest" which remains for believers to enter into (4:3), and the new day appointed by God for this dispensation (4:9), have a new and special foundation, which the previous rests and days had no interest or concern in, namely, that the Author of it ceased from His own works and entered into His rest. Proofs that this verse refers to Christ are many. First, its opening "For," which denotes that the Apostle now indicates whence it is there is a new Sabbatismos remaining for the people of God. He had before shown there could be no such rest but what was founded upon the works of God. Such a foundation this new rest must have, and does have. It is the work of Him by whom the Church is builded: Hebrews 3:3, 4.

Second, the change of number in the pronoun from the plural to the singular intimates the same thing. In Hebrews 4:1-3 the Apostle had used "us" and "we," but here, verse 10, he says, "He that is entered." This is the more noticeable because in the verse immediately preceding he had mentioned "the people of God." That it is not they who are here in view further appears from the fact that they never cease from their works while left in this world. No other reason can possibly be given for this change of number except that a single person is here expressed. Third, note it is not simply said of this person that, "He that is entered into rest" (as in vv. 3 and 8), but "into His rest" absolutely. God spoke of "My rest"; here He mentions "His rest"—Christ's rest!

Fourth, there is a direct parallel supplied by this verse between the works of the old creation and those of the new, which the Apostle is openly comparing together. 1. In the Authors of them: of the former it is said of God the Creator, He did "rest from all His works" (4:4). So "He (Christ) also hath ceased from His own." 2. The products of the One and of the Other are mentioned: Their respective "works," and there is a due proportion between them, each being creative and "very good." 3. There is the rest of the One and of the Other, and these also have a proportion to one another. It should now be unmistakably plain to every impartial reader that it is the Person of Jesus Christ who is the subject spoken of in verse 10.

The blessed Person referred to, then, in verse 10 is the Lord Jesus, and none other—the Author of the new creation. This alone gives meaning to the causal conjunction: there is a Sabbatismos now for the people of God, FOR Christ is entered into His rest. What is denoted by His "rest" we must now inquire. This was certainly not His being in the grave. His body indeed rested there for a brief season, but that was no part of His Mediatory rest, as He is the Builder of His Church; and that for two reasons. First, His entombment was part of His humiliation (Isa. 53:9). Second, the separation of His soul and body was penal, a part of the sentence of the Law which He underwent, and hence Peter declares, "The pains of death" were not loosed until His resurrection (Acts 2:24).

Nor did Christ first enter into His rest at His ascension, rather was that an entrance into His glory, as in the full public manifestation of it. No, Christ's entrance into rest was in, by, and at His resurrection from the dead. For it was then and thereon He was freed from the power and service of the Law, being discharged from the debts of our sins. It was then and thereon that all prefigurations and predictions concerning the work of redemption were fulfilled. It was then and thereon that He received "the promise of the Spirit" (Acts 2:33), and the whole foundation of the Church of God was laid upon His Person. It was then and thereon that He was "declared to be the Son of God with power" (Rom. 1:4). God manifesting unto all that this was He of whom He said, "Thou art My Son, this day have I begotten Thee" (Acts 13:33).

"Thus did the Author of the new creation, the Son of God, having finished His works, enter into His rest. And this was, as we all know, on the morning of the first day of the week. And hereby did He limit and determine the day for a sacred Sabbatical rest under the New Testament. For now was the old covenant (the Siniatic) utterly abolished, and therefore the day which was the pledge of the rest of God and man therein, was to be taken away. As the rest from the beginning of the world had its foundation from the works of God, and His rest which ensued thereon, which was determined unto the seventh day, because that was the day wherein God ceased from those works—which day continued under the legal administration of the covenant by Moses—so the rest of the Lord Christ is the foundation of our rest, which, changing the old covenant, and the day annexed unto it, He hath limited unto the first day of the week, whereon He ceased from His works and entered into His rest.

"Wherefore when the Lord Christ intended conspicuously to build His Church upon the foundation of His works and rest, by sending the Holy Spirit with His miraculous gifts upon the Apostles, He did it on this day: which was then among the Jews the feast of Pentecost. Then were the disciples gathered together with one accord, in the observance of the day signalized to them by His resurrection (Acts 2:1). And by this did their obedience receive a blessed confirmation, as well as their persons a glorious endowment with abilities for the work which they were immediately to apply themselves unto" (John Owen, to whom we are indebted for much in this chapter).

It remains for us to point out that the rest into which Christ entered is proposed unto His people in the Gospel. This is asserted in the precious verse and is here made manifest. "There remaineth therefore a rest [keeping of a Sabbath] to the people of God," (Heb. 4:9) because Christ has entered into His rest. As the other rests—the one at the beginning of human history and the other at the beginning of the commonwealth of Israel—had their foundation in the works and rests of God, whereon a Day of Rest was appointed for them to keep, so has this new rest a foundation in the works and rest of Christ—who has built all things and is God (Heb.

91

3:3, 4), determining a day for our use in and by that whereon He entered into His rest, which is the first day of the week.

Before giving a brief word on verse 11, let us refer to what may present a difficulty unto a few. It should be quite clear there is a Christian Sabbath, a Sabbath appointed for this dispensation. Some may be ready to say, Yes, "for the people of God" (v. 9), but how about unbelievers? First, we answer, we know of nothing in Scripture which intimates that God requires unbelievers to celebrate the first day of the week as a memorial of our Lord's resurrection, for Christ means nothing to them. But second, they are commanded to keep the Sabbath holy unto God their Creator and Ruler. The original Covenant of Works has never been repealed, and all out of Christ are under it. Though the day of Sabbath observance is changed, God requires all alike, believers and unbelievers, to abstain from all secular employment on the Sabbath and keep the day holy unto Himself.

"Let us labour therefore to enter into that rest, lest any man fall after the same example of unbelief" (Heb. 4:11). First, it is to be noted that the Apostle does not here use the term "Sabbatismos" (as in v. 9), but, "katapausis" as in verses 1, 3, 5, etc. This shows that he now returns to his principal exhortation—the reader will be helped on the passage as a whole if he places verses 4-10 in a parenthesis, thus connecting verse 11 with verse 3. In the opening verse of the chapter Paul has said, "Let us therefore fear, lest, a promise being left us of entering into His rest, any of you should seem to come short of it," and here he now makes known how that "fear" is to exert itself. It is not a "fear" of dread or doubt, but is such a reverential respect unto the Divine threats and promises as would stir up its possessors unto all diligence to avoid the one and inherit the other.

The utmost of our endeavours and efforts are required in order to our obtaining an entrance into the rest of Christ. We are to "labour" or give the greatest possible diligence thereto. Men are in real earnest and spend their strength in striving after the bread which perishes; the same intentness and zeal are required in our seeking the Bread of Life. He who teaches men that an entrance into spiritual and eternal rest is a thing plain, easy, and suited to nature, does but delude and deceive them. To mortify sin, deny self, cut off right hands, endure all sorts of afflictions and persecutions— are painful, difficult, and attended with many hardships. The future state of the Christian is one wholly of rest, but his present state is a mixed one, partly of rest and partly of labour—labour against sin, rest in the love and grace of God.

Having now gone carefully through our passage let us see what we have learned from it. First, Hebrews 4 opens with a pointed warning taken from the case of the unbelieving Israelites of old (Heb. 3:16-18). Second, but though those Israelites failed to enter into it, yet there is a rest of God proposed unto us in the Gospel, and which believers enter into (v. 3). Third, this led the Apostle to take up the different "rests" of God and His people: the Edenic, Mosaic, and Messianic (vv. 4-10). Fourth, in leading up to his climax the Apostle throws the emphasis not so much on the "rest" as on the DAY appointed to celebrate it. In verse 7 he declares that God (prophetically) limited or determined "a certain day." In verse 8 he expressly refers to "another day" which supplies proof that a different one from the old seventh day is now instituted. In verse 9 this other day and the rest it memorializes is definitely designated a "Sabbatismos" or "keeping of a Sabbath." In verse 10 he shows why the Sabbath Day had been changed: because it was on that day Christ entered into His rest.

Well, then, may we with the utmost confidence exclaim with the Psalmist, "This is the day which the LORD hath made: we will rejoice and be glad in it" (118:24). "We observe the day as henceforth our true Sabbath, a day made and ordained of God, for the perpetual remembrance of the achievements of our Redeemer" (C. H. Spurgeon). It should be pointed out that the passage we have last quoted is part of a remarkable prophecy, which set forth both the humiliation and exaltation of the Lord Jesus—"the sufferings of Christ and the glory that should follow." The passage is quoted in the New Testament no less than six times, being expressly applied to the Saviour. First, He is seen as "the Stone which the builders refused," and then as "became the Head of the corner" (Psa. 118:2).

And how could that "Stone," contemptuously trodden underfoot by men, become "the Head of the corner"? How indeed except by being raised!? It was by His triumph over death that Christ became the Head of the corner—a "corner" is when two walls meet together, and in resurrection Christ became Head of both believing Jews and believing Gentiles! The Psalmist added, "This is the LORD'S doing, and it is marvellous in our eyes" (Psa. 118:23). And then follows, "This is the day which the LORD hath made." What could be clearer? How perfectly it accords with Hebrews 4:9, 10! That "day" was Divinely "made" to memorialize Christ's victory over the grave: God has "made it remarkable, made it holy, has distinguished it from all other days: it is therefore called the Lord's Day, because it bears His image and superscription" (Matthew Henry).

And so it is: the Christian Sabbath is specifically designated "the Lord's Day" in Revelation 1:10. It is called such because it owes its pre-eminence to the Lord's institution and authority. By taking to Himself the title of "the Lord of the Sabbath" (Mark 2:28), Christ clearly intimated His authority to determine which day of the week a Sabbath rest was to be observed by His people, and by ceasing from His works and entering into His rest on the first day of the week, He has "limited" this one for us. Those who are determined to close their eyes to all this evidence and get rid of the first-day Sabbath at any price, wrest these words in Revelation 1:10 by saying they signify "the Day of the Lord" when He comes in judgment. But the immediate context is dead against them: all that follows from 1:10 to the end of chapter 3 shows that this opening vision respected present and not future things. Moreover, the Greek is different from 2 Peter 3:10! "The

Lord's Supper" (1 Cor. 11:20) memorializes His death; "the Lord's Day" celebrates His resurrection.

Here is a summary of the reasons why Christians should observe the Sabbath on the first day of the week. First, because that day was clearly anticipated by Old Testament typology—the striking things connected with "the eighth day." Second, because the New Covenant necessitated a new Day of rest to signify the old covenant was abrogated. Third, because the honour and glory of Christ required it: on the day specially appointed for Divine worship, God would now have us occupied with His risen and exalted Son. Fourth, His own example bears witness thereto: His repeated meetings with His disciples (John 19) and His sending the Spirit on that day (Acts 2:1) set His imprimatur upon it. Fifth, because the early Church so celebrated it (Acts 20:7; 1 Cor. 16:1, 2). There is not a single recorded instance in the New Testament of the saints meeting together for worship, after Christ's resurrection, on any other day but on the first of the week! Sixth, because we are expressly told that God has "limited" or determined "another day" (Heb. 4:9) than the old one, and that, because Christ then rose from the dead (v. 10). Seventh, because we are Divinely assured that, in view of the raising up of the rejected Stone to be the Head of the corner, "This is the day which the Lord hath made" (Psa. 118:24), and therefore is it called "the Lord's Day" in the New Testament (Rev. 1:10).

7. ITS OBSERVANCE

We have shown that the Sabbath was instituted in Eden, observed by the Patriarchs and renewed at Sinai—and that Israel's prosperity and enjoyment of God's blessings was to a large extent determined by their observance or non-observance of this Divine ordinance. Turning to the New Testament we have seen that Christ expressly affirmed the Sabbath was "made for man" and not for the Jews only, that He is "Lord of the Sabbath" and therefore invested with authority to determine which day of the week shall be sanctified as a holy rest. And we saw in Hebrews 4 the Apostle proves that "another day" than that which obtained under the old covenant has been appointed for its celebration during the Christian era— the first day suitably celebrating the Saviour's entrance into His mediatorial rest. This is demonstrated by the practice of the early Church (Acts 20:7; 1 Cor. 16:1, 2).

We are now to consider the all-important matter of how the Sabbath is to be kept. The chief end of God's Word and of all instruction therein is that the doctrinal principles which it enunciates may direct us unto a performance suited thereto. The light which we receive from the Living Oracle lays upon us a binding obligation to walk accordingly. Doctrine must regulate deportment. This was the Grand Rule laid down by the Supreme Teacher: "If ye know these things, happy are ye if ye do them" (John 13:17). The design of our learning Scripture Truth is for us to obtain such an understanding thereof that conduct accordant therewith may be produced. Where there is knowledge without the corresponding discharge of duty, the truth is held "in unrighteousness" (Rom. 1:18), and then double is our guilt. Practice must conform to the precept.

It is, then, to the practical side of our subject we now turn: may Divine wisdom be so granted us that we are preserved from going to an undue extreme either on the right hand or on the left. No one who is acquainted with human nature or who is conversant with the history and literature on this branch of our subject, can honestly doubt there is a real danger of failing to preserve the balance here—as everywhere. On the one hand care must be taken lest in our zeal for the sanctity and spirituality of the Sabbath we go to an excess in multiplying rules for its observance, and thereby fall into the Pharisaic error of rigour and excess. On the other hand, there is a far greater danger today of erring on the side of laxity and of accommodating the laws regulating this institution to the lusts of the flesh and yielding to the corrupt practices of an evil and adulterous generation.

The strict requirements of God's holiness must be insisted upon, no matter how the world scoffs at or opposes them. As these very lines are being written [1939] God is manifesting His displeasure at the increasing desecration of His holy rest-day by disturbing the rest of Christendom—those nations which have enjoyed most of the privileges of the Gospel—being seriously threatened with war. And the blame for this widespread desecration rests first and chiefly upon the churches: by the banishing of the Law from its pulpits, by the feeble or total lack of protest to legislative bodies for letting down the bars and legalizing the profanation of the Lord's Day, and by the general worldliness of its members. It is therefore high time that Christian leaders should faithfully expound the Fourth Commandment and cease accommodating it to the perverse wills and ways of the ungodly.

Sad, indeed, is the declension in genuine piety. The foundations have been forsaken, standards have been lowered, the spirit of compromise has prevailed until, now, "Truth is fallen in the streets." Nor can the apostasy be checked by temporizing the commands of God to the corrupt course of the world. Yet we must beware of adding to those commands. Said the Puritan Owen, "I will not deny but that there have been and are mistakes in this matter. Directions have been given, and that not by a few, for the observance of a day of holy rest, which either for the matter of them or the manner prescribed, have had no sufficient warrant or foundation in the Scriptures. For whereas some have made no distinction between the Sabbath as moral and as Mosaic, unless it be merely in the change of the day, they have endeavoured to introduce the whole practice required on the latter into the Lord's Day."

How is a happy medium in Sabbath observance to be obtained? What will preserve us from undue laxity on the one side, and unwarrantable severity on the other? Where shall we turn for that much-needed guidance which will deliver us from the grievous yoke of Pharisaical excess, and which will also prevent us from degenerating into the lawlessness of our Moderns? We have searched long and diligently for a satisfactory answer to this question, but (amid much that was helpful on other branches of our subject) have failed to meet with anything clear and definite. Personally our firm conviction is that we shall be kept from going wrong in this matter, if we, first, adhere strictly to the letter of the Fourth Commandment; and second, apply that commandment to the details of our lives in the spirit of the New Covenant.

It should be apparent that we have now arrived at the most important branch of our subject. Unless both writer and reader are genuinely and earnestly desirous of keeping the Sabbath in a manner which will be pleasing to the Lord and beneficial to the soul, then all our previous efforts to prove that this Divine ordinance is binding upon us today, will avail little or nothing. But the task before us now is no easy one: our chief difficulty being the avoidance of too great editing on the one hand, and too much brevity on the other. We do not wish to extend this book to the point of wearying our friends, yet we must not abbreviate so much that we withhold the help which is desired upon various problems that exercise not a few. Some have had no instruction upon Sabbath observance: others have been given so many rules to follow that a spirit of bondage has been engendered. We shall therefore endeavour to steer a middle course.

Taking Exodus 20:8-11 as our starting point, we note first that that which outstandingly characterizes this season is its sacredness: "Remember the Sabbath Day to keep it holy." This is basic and foremost. It is "the Lord's Day," being instituted for His honour and glory. God, by the appointing and blessing of it, has made this day: we, by the worship of Him and performance of spiritual exercises therein, are to keep it holy. And let it be carefully borne in mind that holiness pertains not only to external actions, but also and mainly to the spring from which they proceed, namely, the heart: unless we sanctify the Sabbath in our hearts, the performing of outward devotions will avail us nothing As the other six days are concerned mainly with secular things, the seventh is to be consecrated unto spiritual ends. Holiness stands opposed not only to all that is sinful, but also to the use of such things (our time and energy) as are commonly employed.

"Remember the Sabbath Day to keep it holy": not a part thereof, but the whole of it. In all countries where Romanism dominates, its deluded votaries spend a part of the morning in religious exercises, and for the balance of the day give themselves up to feasting and pleasuring. Sad to say this evil is becoming more and more rife in Protestant circles: though we may not yet have gone to the same lengths of profanity as is general "on the Continent," yet thousands in this land who attend some morning service, spend the afternoon and evening in making social calls on their friends, car riding, and other fleshly and worldly activities. It is this unholy mixture, this "lukewarmness"—being neither hot nor cold—which is so nauseating to the Lord. Because it is the Lord's Day, we rob Him of His due if we regard any part of it as ours.

The second thing we note in Exodus 20:8-11 is that the Sabbath is expressly affirmed to be a day of rest: "the seventh day is the Sabbath of the LORD thy God: in it thou shalt not do any work." That prohibition is qualified (as the example and teaching of Christ made clear) at two points only: the doing of that which is really essential to life and health, and engaging in acts of love and mercy. Apart from those exceptions, all work and labour—be it manual or clerical, physical or mental—is Divinely forbidden. And this, as was pointed out earlier, is a merciful provision of the Creator for His creatures. Continuous toil is injurious to our constitution. "The Sabbath was made for man," for his well-being, because he needed one day of rest in each week. This law is as binding upon and holds good for the wife equally as for the husband, for the servant as much as his master, yea, for his beasts of burden too.

This law is as binding upon our private lives as upon our public, upon the way in which we conduct ourselves within the home as on the outside. It is just as real a profanation of the Holy Sabbath for a merchant to cast up his ledger or write business letters on that day, as for a farmer to go out and plow his fields or sow corn. So, too, is it equally sinful for his wife to prepare and cook elaborate meals on the Lord's Day as it would be for her to do her weekly washing and ironing then. Nor can this be evaded—as many seem to suppose—by the mistress accompanying her husband to the morning service and leaving her daughter or maid to cook the biggest dinner of the week. Alas, in many homes, not only does the cook have no rest on the Lord's Day, but it is the heaviest one of the week for her.

Let us next point out that there is a positive side to the Fourth Commandment as well as a negative. Not only are we to abstain from all worldly business, but we are to be active in spiritual exercises. A day spent in idleness is not one which is kept holy. The Day of Rest is not to be one of indolence, but one of blessed and sacred diligence. Physical rest is necessary, but spiritual rest is yet more essential. In its higher aspect, true Sabbatical rest is the soul resting in the Lord. This is evident from the fact that the Sabbath is both an emblem and a pledge of the eternal rest of the saints, concerning which it is said "His servants shall serve Him" (Rev. 22:3), which means that they will be actively engaged in His worship. Inasmuch then as the duties of this day are eminently spiritual, they are such as lie beyond our own powers to perform, and therefore we must seek the aid of the Holy Spirit.

A third thing we should observe is that the Sabbath is to be a season of rejoicing: "This is the day which the LORD hath made: we will rejoice and be glad in it" (Psa. 118:24). The immediate context contains a grand Messianic prophecy, wherein the triumph of Christ was set forth. Under the figure of "the Stone," He is viewed first, in His humiliation, as despised and rejected by men, as being refused by the builders. Next He is portrayed in His glorification, as owned and honoured of God, as being made "The Headstone of the corner." The exaltation of Christ was in three stages: when He was raised from the tomb, when He ascended to Heaven, and when He sat down at the right hand of the Majesty on high. "This is the LORD'S doing: it is marvellous in our eyes" (v. 23). The exaltation of Christ was wholly of the Lord: the product of His eternal counsel, the product of His mighty power; and it is the subject of never-ceasing wonderment to His redeemed.

"This is the day which the LORD hath made," and therefore it is peculiarly and pre-eminently "the Lord's Day," and so it is expressly denominated in Revelation 1:10. It is the day which the Lord made specially for this Christian dispensation, namely, the first of the week. It is the day which has been made forever memorable by loosing the Redeemer from the pains of death. It is now the day in which His people are to celebrate the Saviour's victory over the sepulchre. And therefore Christians must exclaim, "we will rejoice and be glad in it": not only because of its appointment, but because of its occasion, for Christ's resurrection was both for His own honour and for our salvation. Holy mirth, then, should fill our hearts at this season: Sabbath Days ought to be unto us as foretastes of Heaven itself. Then let us welcome each weekly return of it, and duly tune our hearts to show forth His praises therein.

The order of Truth in the passage last quoted, is the order we must observe if we are to enter experimentally therein. We shall be glad and rejoice in proportion as our hearts are truly occupied with the risen Redeemer and of our being risen in Him. As Spurgeon well put it, "What else can we do? Having obtained so great a deliverance through our illustrious Leader, and having seen the eternal mercy of God so brilliantly displayed, it would ill become us to mourn and murmur. Rather will we exhibit a double joy, rejoice in heart and be glad in face, rejoice in secret and be glad in public, for we have more than a double reason for being glad in the Lord. We ought to especially rejoice on the Sabbath: it is the queen of days, and its hours should be clad in royal apparel of delight."

What abundant cause have we for rejoicing therein! The resurrection of Christ marked the end of His inexpressible humiliation, and signaled the beginning of His unending glorification. It demonstrated that He had made an end of sins, effected reconciliation for iniquity, and brought in everlasting righteousness (Dan. 9:24). It affords proof of God's approval of the Mediator's work and the acceptance of His sacrifice. It meant that the whole Election of Grace were delivered from death and Hell when their federal Head became "alive for evermore." The resurrection of Christ is both the pledge and the prototype of the resurrection of His sleeping people. "If ye then be risen with Christ, seek those things which are above" (Col. 3:1). And what are those things which are above? Spiritual rest, spiritual joy—complete deliverance from our warfare with sin, unalloyed rejoicing in the Lord. Then "seek" them: by the actings of faith, by the exercise of hope, by the outgoings of love. We should have a double enjoyment of the things above: by anticipation now, by realization then.

The same keynote is struck in the first stanza of Psalm 92. It is to be noted that the inspired heading to this Psalm is, "A Song for the Sabbath." And what is its opening theme? This, "It is a good thing to give thanks unto the LORD, and to sing praises unto Thy name, O Most High: To show forth

Thy lovingkindness in the morning, and Thy faithfulness every night. Upon an instrument of ten strings, and upon the psaltery; upon the harp with a solemn sound. For Thou, LORD, hast made me glad through Thy work: I will triumph in the works of Thy hands. O LORD, how great are Thy works; and Thy thoughts are very deep" (vv. 1-5). Praise is Sabbatical work: the joyfulness of hearts resting in the Lord. Since a true Sabbath can only be found in God, it is essential that we be supremely occupied with His perfections on that day.

We have pointed out that the essential principles which should regulate us in the keeping of the Sabbath Day holy are a strict compliance with the letter of the Fourth Commandment and the discharge of the same in the spirit of the New Covenant. It seems to us that such a combination will best enable to preserve the balance, delivering us on the one hand from unwarrantable laxity, and on the other from undue rigour and Pharisaic excess. While it is to be emphatically insisted upon that the Moral Law is as much binding on us today as ever it was upon the Jews, yet it must also be as unmistakably affirmed that the Christian receives the Law not from Moses but from the hands of Christ. It is not the irksome tasks of slaves, but the ready and joyous service of sons and daughters which God asks from believers.

It should be the diligent concern of the Christian to observe the Sabbath Day and to perform the duties required therein with a frame of mind becoming God's dear children, and in a spirit answering to the freedom and liberty of the Gospel. We are to serve God in all things "in newness of spirit and not in the oldness of the letter" (Rom. 7:6). That is to say, our obedience and worship is to be rendered unto God with a spirit of grace, joy, liberty, and a sound mind—and not in that darkness, dread, and servility which characterized the old covenant. In contrast from the blessed liberty wherewith Christ makes believers free, that which marked Judaism was a bondage frame of mind, so that their observance of the duties of the Law, and consequently of the Sabbath, were rendered in a servile spirit.

The Puritan John Owen pointed out three things tending thereto. First, the dreadful giving of the Law on Sinai. The fearful phenomena which accompanied the promulgation of the Law at that time was designed to strike terror not only into the generation who immediately witnessed it, but also throughout all generations of the Mosaic economy to awe the hearts of Israel with a dread and terror of it. In proof of this we find the Apostle declaring plainly that Mount Sinai "gendereth to bondage" (Gal. 4:24). It was the very nature of Judaism to bring its subjects into a spiritually servile state, and consequently although secretly on account of the ends of the covenant they were children and heirs, yet "they differed nothing from servants" (Gal. 4:1-3). It is the grand dispensational change brought in by Christ that is treated of in Galatians 4.

Again—the re-enforcement of the Adamic Covenant, with the promise and threat of it, necessarily produced the same effect upon the nation of Israel, for that covenant was binding upon them throughout the whole continuance of Judaism. True, the Moral Law had a new use and end given unto it at Sinai, yet those who received it were so much in the dark and the proposal of that new end and use was attended with so great an obscurity, that they could not look unto the comfort and liberty which was to be the grand outcome. "The Law made nothing perfect," and what was of grace in the administration of it was so veiled under typical ceremonies and shadows that they could not behold "the end" or design of that which was to be abolished (2 Cor. 3:13)—where the same grand dispensational change is also discussed.

Finally, the affixing of the death penalty to the Law increased this bondage. The grim prospect of death overshadowing disobedience would obviously inspire their service with terror, and this is exactly what it was designed to express and produce, so as to represent the original curse of the whole

Law (Gal. 3:13). Thereby the majority of them were greatly awed and terrified, though a few of them, by special grace, were enabled to delight themselves in God and His holy ordinances. By these things, then, was administered a "spirit of bondage to fear," which by the Apostle is opposed to "the spirit of adoption, whereby we cry Abba Father" (Rom. 8:15). From those things arose the many anxious scruples which were upon them in the observance of the Sabbath. Though they boasted they were the children of Abraham and never in bondage, yet the Saviour insisted that, whatever they pretended, they were not free until the Son should make them free (John 8:36).

If it were needful for the Apostle to remind the believing Hebrews that they did not go to Sinai, but to Mount Sion, to receive the Law, it is requisite that believers be taught the same today. "For ye are not come unto the mount that might be touched, and that burned with fire, nor unto blackness and darkness and tempest, and the sound of a trumpet, and the voice of words; which voice they that heard entreated that the words should not be spoken to them any more: (for they could not endure that which was commanded, and if so much as a beast touched the mountain, it shall be stoned, or thrust through with a dart: and so terrible was the sight, that Moses said, I exceedingly fear and quake.) But ye are come unto Mount Sion and unto the city of the living God, the heavenly Jerusalem . . . and to Jesus the Mediator of the new covenant, and to the blood of sprinkling that speaketh better things than that of Abel" (Heb. 12:18-24).

Under the Gospel, Christians are delivered from all the terror-provoking considerations which brought the Jews into such spiritual bondage. They are connected with a radically different order of things, for "Jerusalem which is above is free, which is the mother of us all" (Gal. 4:26), which is but another way of saying that we receive the Law of our obedience from Jesus Christ, who speaks from Mount Sion, and who is to be heeded with a filial spirit of liberty (cf. Gal. 5:1). So far as Christians are concerned the

Adamic covenant is absolutely abolished, nor is the remembrance of it anyway revived (Heb. 8:13), so that it should have any influence upon their minds. They have been taken into a Covenant full of peace and joy, for "The law was given by Moses, but grace and truth came by Jesus Christ" (John 1:17).

In the Covenant of Grace we receive the spirit of Christ or adoption to serve God without legal fear (Luke 1:74; Rom. 8:15; Gal. 4:6), and there is not anything more insisted on in the Gospel as the principal privilege thereof. Nor would it be of any account to have liberty in the word and rule, if we had it not in the spirit and principle. It is by this Gospel liberty we are delivered from that anxious solicitude about particular instances in outward duties, which was a great part of the yoke imposed by the system of Judaism. It is most important and needful that this principle of evangelical freedom be insisted upon (for though the Fall has made us prone unto lawlessness, yet by nature we are also essentially legalistic), otherwise one of the most vital and fundamental elements of the Gospel will be submerged.

In all his duties, the Christian should look upon God as his Father, for through Christ both believing Jews and believing Gentiles have "access in one spirit unto the Father" (Eph. 2:18). Our Father is not One who will "always chide," nor does He "watch our steps" for our hurt. He is not One who binds upon us a grievous burden, but "knoweth our frame and remembereth that we are dust" (Psa. 103:14). He does not tie us down to rigid exactness in outward things, while we act in a holy spirit of filial obedience as His children. There is a vast difference between the duties of servants and sons, as there is between obeying a master and a parent. The consideration and application of this principle if it be regulated by the general rules laid down in the Word will resolve a thousand such scruples as perplexed the Jews of old.

Let it also be observed that our Father requires to be worshipped "in spirit and in truth" (John 4:24). He has far more respect to the inward frame of our hearts wherewith we serve Him, than He does to the mere outward performance of duties. The latter can only be accepted by Him as they are the expressions and demonstrations thereof. If, then, in our observance of the Holy Sabbath our hearts are single and sincere in our desires for His glory with delight, it is of more price with Him than the most rigid and punctilious observance of external duties by number and measure. "It hath been no small mistake that men have laboured more to multiply directions about external duties, giving them out as it were by number or tale, than to direct the inward man unto a due performance of the whole duty of the sanctification of the day according to the spirit and genius of Gospel obedience" (John Owen, to whom we are indebted for much of the above).

Here, then, is the essential difference between the Judaical and the Christian Sabbath: the minds of believers are no longer influenced to the duties of its observance by the curse of the Law and the terror thereof as represented in the threatened penalty of death. Instead it is love for the Person of Jesus Christ and respect for His authority which are the springs of their obedience. This cannot be insisted upon too strongly, for it marks the difference between a slavish and filial compliance. Consequently our main duty lies in an endeavour to obtain spiritual joy and delight in the services of this Day, as these are the special effects of spiritual liberty. Nor will this be difficult to attain if we are actively engaged in the privileges and blessings of the Gospel: the actings of faith upon the benefits secured for us by Christ cannot fail to produce deeper devotion, for faith ever works by love.

In what has been pointed out above we are far from joining hands with those who belittle the sanctity of the Lord's Day and who contend that they are so delivered from the Law that they are free to please themselves (within the limitations of decency) as to how they show their respect for this ordinance. There is a world of difference between spiritual liberty and fleshly license. Those whom Christ makes free are freed Godwards and not sinwards. The Rule of obedience is the same for those who are now under the New Covenant as it was for those under the Old: it is the spring from which obedience proceeds which is altered. Then, it was the obedience of servants in terror of death for disobedience; now, it is the worship of sons out of gratitude to a loving Father.

Our first and chief concern must be to diligently see to it that the Lord is not robbed by us of any part of His due on the Sabbath Day; yet care needs also to be taken that we are not brought under bondage to "the commandments and doctrines of men." It has to be admitted that some, with a zeal which was not according to knowledge, felt that the sanctification of the Lord's Day could best be secured by multiplying the duties of piety. Accordingly, they drew up excessive directions regarding the same, both proscribing and prescribing that which lacked Scriptural authority for the same under the Gospel. When such a strictness is required that the saints cannot come up to it with a delight therein, then we may rightly suspect that the requirements laid down by God have been exceeded, and the inevitable result will be a swinging to the opposite extreme of laxity.

We cannot improve upon the ways of the Lord, and any attempt to do so must inevitably meet with failure. It is just as foolish to go beyond the Rule which He has given us, as it is wrong for us to come short thereof. Where He has particularized we must not generalize, and where He has only generalized we should not dogmatically particularize. Is it not at this very point that one of the most outstanding differences between the two economies is to be found? Under the Mosaic God furnished detailed laws for the Jews to heed—laws which pertained to every phase of their lives— but under the Christian He has, in many instances, supplied us only with general principles for the regulation of our conduct. Considerable latitude is allowed us in the application of those principles to particular instances —as is clear from such passages as Romans 14:1-9; 1 Corinthians 8:8-9, etc. Those, then, who are not content with urging unto a compliance with such general principles, and instead, draw up a full code of specific regulations are contravening the genius of Christianity and inculcating the spirit of Judaism.

In order to prevent misunderstanding at this point, we call attention to one or two of the general principles enunciated in the Epistles, to which we must ever turn for full-orbed Christianity. "Whether therefore ye eat, or drink, or whatsoever ye do, do all to the glory of God" (1 Cor. 10:31). Here is expressed the fundamental principle for the regulating of practical godliness: this is the grand rule which is ever to guide us where express precepts are not supplied—self is to be denied and the eye fixed on God alone, so that we aim at honouring Him in everything. "Let all things be done decently and in order" (1 Cor. 14:40). This is the general rule to regulate us in all the details of public worship as the former concerned more directly our domestic or private lives. It is a simple principle which, if heeded, will furnish guidance on many matters of church life concerning which the New Testament does not specifically legislate.

"Let all your things be done with charity" (1 Cor. 16:14). If this were duly attended to, how many disputes would be avoided, ill-feelings spared, and difficulties solved? All our affairs, domestically and ecclesiastically, should be regulated by love. Earnestness must not degenerate into bitterness, nor firmness into tyranny. If zeal be governed by love then excesses and cruelty will be obviated. "Whatsoever ye do, do it heartily as to the Lord, and not unto men" (Col. 3:23). Here is yet another general principle, which is to govern us in all our undertakings: our service is not to be forced but spontaneous, rendered not grudgingly but gladly. It will be noted that the chief emphasis in these general principles is thrown upon the inward springs of action rather than upon the outward performances themselves, and that they afford room for the exercise of sanctified common sense, moral instincts, and Spiritual intuitions.

"If thou turn away thy foot from the Sabbath, from doing thy pleasure on My holy day; and call the Sabbath a delight, the holy of the LORD, honourable; and shalt honour Him, not doing thine own ways, nor finding thine own pleasure, nor speaking thine own words: Then shalt thou delight thyself in the LORD; and I will cause thee to ride upon the high places of the earth, and feed thee with the heritage of Jacob thy father" (Isa. 58:13, 14). This is one of the many Old Testament predictions which relates chiefly to Gospel times—the section in which it occurs clearly denoting this, coming as it does after the death of Christ in Chapter 53. In it we may clearly discern the two leading principles which we have contended for throughout this article: the maintenance of the letter of the Fourth Commandment, and a compliance therewith in the spirit of the New Covenant. While there is much greater liberty under the Christian economy than there was under the Mosaic, yet the standard of holiness is not lowered nor are the requirements of God waived.

"If thou turn away thy foot from the Sabbath." This, it seems to us, has a twofold force: a general and a specific—if you refrain from trampling upon it, and if you abstain from journeying and gadding about on that Day. The opening clause is explained by, "from doing thy pleasure on My holy day": fleshly indulgence is no more permissible now than it was under the old covenant. This prohibition is specified in three details: "not doing thine own ways nor finding thine own pleasure, nor speaking thine own words." The Lord's Day is not to be spent in seeking our secular interests, nor by engaging in worldly recreations, nor by vain and trifling conversation. Positively, we are to "call the Sabbath a delight, the holy of the Lord, honourable," which agree with Psalm 118:24. The reward for such obedience (v. 14) must be understood of New Testament blessings expressed in Old Testament terminology.

"If thou turn away thy foot from the Sabbath, from doing thy pleasure on My holy day; and call the Sabbath a delight, the holy of the LORD, honourable; and shalt honour Him, not doing thine own ways, nor finding thine own pleasure, nor speaking thine own words" (Isa. 58:13). We quote this passage again because it sums up what we have sought to bring before the reader. First, it expresses the grand truth that the Sabbath is not to be looked upon as an irksome duty, but as a sacred privilege. Instead of being a burden grievous to be borne, it affords us a special opportunity for profitable and joyous exercises. The spirit in which we are to enter upon its hallowed employments is neither one of bondage nor dread, but of freedom and gladness. We are to find in it our greatest joy of the week, delighting ourselves in the Lord, all that is within us praising His holy name.

The accompanying promises afford great encouragement for those whose sincere desire it is to honour the Lord in this ordinance: "Then shalt thou delight thyself in the LORD; and I will cause thee to ride upon the high places of the earth, and feed thee with the heritage of Jacob thy father: for the mouth of the LORD hath spoken it" (v. 14). Expressed in New Covenant terms, that means, first, such an observance of the Sabbath will afford us much more comfort in the Lord. "The more pleasure we take in serving God, the more pleasure we shall find in it. If we go about duty cheerfully, we shall go from it with satisfaction" (Matthew Henry). Second, we shall be given victory over our spiritual enemies: observe how the Lord's causing Israel to triumph over the Egyptians is spoken of as, "He made him ride on the high places of the earth" (Deut. 32:13). Third, our souls shall be richly fed with the blessings of the covenant. The precious products of the antitypical Canaan—fed with foretastes of it now.

Having fully established the two basic principles which are to regulate us in Sabbath observance, we must now point out something of the practical application of the same to the details of this duty. First, we will consider the preparation which should be made, for we cannot enter properly or profitably into the keeping of this holy rest without a fit approach thereto. It is noteworthy that this expression, "the preparation, that is, the day before the Sabbath" (Mark 15:42) occurs not in the Old Testament but in the New, being found in substance in each of the four Gospels. This sacred institution is not to be approached lightly and carelessly, but with definite forethought and conscientious preparation of our secular affairs, our domestic arrangements, and especially of our hearts. We greatly fear that it is failure at this very point which is the reason why so many miss the richest benefits of this ordinance.

Before proceeding further we must carefully consider the question as to when this "preparation" is to begin, and this requires us to fix the time at which the Sabbath itself commences. In certain quarters this has been made a point of controversy, some contending that it begins at sunset of the preceding day and ends with sunset of its own, appealing to, "from even unto even shall ye celebrate your Sabbath" (Lev. 23:32). That this was one noteworthy feature of and obtained throughout the Mosaic economy is readily granted, but that the same is binding on us today we emphatically deny. In the first place, a day of rest, according to the rules of natural equity, ought to be proportioned unto a day of work, and that is reckoned both in the Old Testament and in the New Testament as from morning to evening: Psalm 104:20-23; Matthew 20:1-8.

In the second place, our Lord Jesus Christ, who in His resurrection gave beginning and being to the special Day of holy rest under the Gospel, came forth from the grave not until the morning of the first day of the week, when the light of the sun began to dispel the darkness of the night, or when it dawned towards the day, as it is variously expressed by the Evangelists. This should settle the matter for His people. Thus, the Christian Sabbath is again sharply distinguished from the Judaical Sabbath. Finally, it should be pointed out that in the description furnished of the first seven days of Genesis 1, that while it is said of each of the first six that it was constituted of an evening and a morning, yet of the seventh this is significantly omitted: it is simply called "the seventh day," without any mention of the preceding evening. Thus the Mosaic was distinguished from the primitive Sabbath as well as from the Christian.

Our Sabbath. then, is to be regarded as extending from midnight of the seventh day (Saturday) till midnight of the first day. Thus the "preparation" for it would fall upon the Saturday, particularly the evening of that day. "Remember the Sabbath Day to keep it holy," includes the taking of all necessary forethought which is required for the sanctifying thereof. It is a profanation of the Lord's Day to make it one of feasting, and therefore its meals should be as plain and simple as possible, and all cooking done on Saturday (Exo. 16:23). The women who cared for our Lord's body mixed the spices and ointments on the day preceding, considering it a servile work not suitable for the Sabbath (Luke 23:54, 56). Has not this been recorded for our learning?

The due preparation of our hearts and minds is especially needful. As we are to keep our foot when going to the house of God (Eccl. 5:1), that is, consider what we are about to do, to where we are going, and that which is due God in our solemn approaches unto Him; so we must not enter into the sacred exercises of His holy day without thought and prayer. "I will be sanctified in them that draw nigh Me" (Lev. 10:3) is the Lord's unwavering requirement. He is greatly dishonoured when we carelessly rush into any of the appointed means of grace, and therefore does the Apostle exhort us, "Let us have grace whereby we may serve God acceptably, with reverence and godly fear" (Heb. 12:28). This means far more than grave countenances and bodily postures of veneration: let us have hearts and minds that are spiritualized.

Our first concern should be to see to it that our minds are freed from the worries of business and the cares of this life, so that they may without distraction be staved upon the Lord. Much converse with the world is very apt to beget a worldly frame of mind in us, and being so much absorbed with earthly things during the six working days taints the heart with worldliness. Though it be our duty in all our secular concerns to live unto God therein and do everything unto His glory, yet they exert such an influence upon us as to unfit us for spiritual exercises and heavenly contemplation. And therefore it devolves upon us to purge our minds of secular affairs, business concerns, and worldly cares, as far as in us lies, so that we may the better and more wholly rest in and delight ourselves with the Lord.

In endeavouring to bring our souls into a fit frame for the duties of the Lord's Day, the evening before we should engage our thoughts with meditations suitable thereto. This is a fitting time to consider the lost Sabbaths of our unregenerate days, and which we have to account for or repent of. This is the time to review the week now nearly ended, and put right with God our sad failures therein. Then is the time to meditate upon the wondrous patience of God, which has so long borne with our waywardness and slackness, and who notwithstanding has spared us to approach another Sabbath. This is the time to ponder the vanity of worldly things and how utterly contemptible they are when compared with communion with God. This is the time to give ourselves up to confession, to prayer, to praise.

As our eyes open upon the light of the Sabbath we should most earnestly pray that we may be preserved from trifling away its holy hours, and seriously should we ask ourselves how we may most profitably improve them. We ought to be very importunate with God that He will graciously banish from our minds everything which would distract and turn us away from Him, that He would so sanctify our hearts that from the beginning to the end of His day we may be entirely given up to those ends and exercises for which He has consecrated the Sabbath. We ought also to be equally importunate in praying that He will grant His ministers the assistance of the Holy Spirit in preparing a message which will glorify Him and edify His people. So, too, we should ask the Lord for the same spiritual mercies to be bestowed upon our fellow-saints as we have craved for ourselves. This will serve to prepare us to engage in family devotions, before we wait upon the public worship of the day.

Throughout the Sabbath we are to abstain from everything that would impede its spiritual observance. Under no circumstances must there be any buying or selling on that Day, or the encouraging of those who do so. Sunday newspapers and all secular literature is to be then strictly banned by us. The paying of social calls and the making of unnecessary visits whereby the worship of God in families is interrupted and worldly conversation is introduced are desecrations of the Sabbath. All unnecessary work in providing for our dining tables on that day is to be avoided: a cold meal with God's blessing is infinitely better than a hot one with His frown. Great watchfulness must be exercised against idle conversation. "Let no corrupt communication proceed out of your mouth, but that which is good to the use of edifying, that it may minister grace unto the hearers" (Eph. 4:29)—that holds good at all times, but doubly so on the Sabbath.

All needless taking of journeys on the Lord's Day are sinful. In this connection we would earnestly remind the reader of that exhortation of Christ's, "But pray ye that your flight be not in the winter, neither on the Sabbath Day" (Matt. 24:20). This was plainly a prophetic warning against that species of Sabbath desecration which has, alas, become so rife. It is rendered the more striking inasmuch as it is the only warning He gave to His disciples against any particular kind of encroachment on the Day of Rest. And for what does He here teach them to pray? Not that they may be kept from travelling for pleasure or for purposes of commerce, but that in a time of calamity and danger events might be so ordered by God that they should not be obliged to preserve their lives and flee for safety by travelling on that day. How He wished to impress upon us the unique sanctity of the Sabbath!

Turning now to the positive side: the reading and pondering of the Scripture should have a prominent place in the occupations of this Day. In our strenuous age there are comparatively few who have many leisure hours through the week, and often they are too weary to use those they do have for serious study. But it is far otherwise on the Day of Rest: special opportunity is then afforded for seeking spiritual nourishment. At least one hour in the early morning, another in the afternoon, and one more before retiring, ought to be spent in the Word of God and devotional literature. As six days have been directed mainly to providing for the needs of the body, the seventh is to be improved by seeking food for the soul: thereby is our strength renewed and we are fitted for the duties of the ensuing week.

In addition to seasons of private prayer and feeding on the Word, all our spare moments on the Lord's Day should be employed in spiritual meditations. Then is our golden opportunity for serious reflections and delightful contemplation: to turn our thoughts from things temporal to things spiritual, and to project our minds into that eternal state to which we are constantly approaching. We should meditate on God as Creator and delight ourselves afresh in all His wondrous works. We should consider how we lost our original rest in God by sin, and how He might justly have abandoned us to eternal restlessness. We should meditate upon the recovery of our rest in God by the great atonement of Christ and His triumphant emerging from the grave. This is indeed the principal duty of this day: to dwell upon and rejoice in this recovery of a rest in God and of a rest for God in us. This is the fruit of infinite wisdom, amazing grace, and incomprehensible love: then let us give glory to God and His Christ for the same. We are also to remember that the Sabbath is a pledge of our everlasting rest with God.

Let it also be observed that this Day affords the most favourable opportunity for training children in the fear and nurture of the Lord. Family instruction is one of the most important duties thereof. How many thousands owe their conversion, under God, to Sabbath catechising, Scripture reading, and religious instruction, and the simple but fervent prayers of a pious parent or relative! The heads of families should do all they can to promote the spiritual and eternal good of those under their care. No Christian parent should entrust the instructing of his children in the things of God to only Sunday School teachers, but ought to personally discharge much of this responsibility. Let portions of the Word be read together, simple explanations and practical applications be made: verses should be allotted for memorizing during the week, with a hearing of the same on the Sabbath. Such books as Bunyan's Pilgrim's Progress, the life of some Missionary, etc., may also be profitably read to the children.

This is also a season eminently suitable for works of charity. All possible doubt on this score has been removed by the specific teaching and personal example of Christ. He affirmed that it is lawful to do well on the Sabbath Day. It is both our privilege and duty, especially of those without family responsibilities, to seek after and minister unto those who are cut off from the public means of grace: to visit the sick and the aged, to read the Word to those who cannot read it for themselves, to engage in acts of mercy and compassion unto those needing our help. The more we endeavour to brighten the lot of others, the more will we enter into the joy of Him who ever went about doing good. It is always the self-centered who are the most discontented and miserable.

We heartily endorse the following observations from the Puritan, Owen. "There is no such certain standard or measure for the observance of the duties of this day, as that every one who exceeds it should by it be cut short, or that those who on important reasons come short of it should be stretched out thereunto. As God provided in His services of old that he who was not able to offer a bullock might offer a dove, with respect unto their outward condition in the world, so here there is an allowance also for the natural temperaments and abilities of men. Only whereas if persons of old had pretended poverty to save their charge in the procuring of an offering, it would not have been acceptable, yea, they would themselves have fallen under the curse of the deceiver; so no more now will a pretence of weakness or natural inability be an excuse for any neglect or profaneness. Otherwise, God requires of us and accepts from us according to what we have, and not according to what we have not.

"We see it by experience that some men's natural spirits will carry them to a continuance in the outward observance of duties much beyond, nay, doubly perhaps to what others are able, who yet may observe the holy Sabbath to the Lord with acceptation. And herein lies the spring of the accommodation of these duties to the sick, the aged, the young, the weak, or persons any way distempered. God 'knoweth our frame and remembereth we are dust,' so also that the dust is more discomposed and weakly compacted in some than others. As thus the people gathered manna of old, some more, some less, 'every man according to his appetite,' yet he that gathered much had nothing over, and he that gathered little had no lack' (Exo. 16:17-18). So is everyone in sincerity, according to his own ability, to endeavour the sanctifying of the name of God in the duties of this day, not being obliged by the examples or prescriptions of others, according to their own measures."

Commenting on the cautions of Isaiah 58:13 Owen said, "I no way think that here is a restraint laid on us from such words, ways and works, as neither hinder the performance of any religious duties belonging to the due celebration of the worship of God on His day, nor are apt in themselves to unframe our spirits or divert our affections from them. And those whose minds are fixed in a spirit of liberty to glorify God in and by this day of rest, seeking after communion with Him in the ways of His worship, will be to themselves a better rule for their words and actions, than those who may aim to reckon over all they do or say, which may be done in such a manner as to become the Judaical Sabbath much more than the Lord's Day.

"Although the day be wholly to be dedicated to the ends of a sacred rest before insisted on, yet duties in their performance drawn out to such a length as to beget wearisomeness tend not to edification, nor promote the sanctification of the name of God in the worship itself. Regard, therefore, in all such performances is to be had unto the weakness of the natural constitution of some, the infirmities and indisposition of others, who are not able to abide in the outward part of duties as others can. And there is no wise shepherd who will rather suffer the stronger sheep of his flock to lose somewhat of what they might reach to in his guidance of them, than to compel the weaker to keep pace with them to their hurt, and it may be to their ruin. Better a great number should complain of the shortness of some duties, who have strength and desires for a longer continuance in them, than that a few who are sincere should be really discouraged by being overburdened, and have the service thereby made useless to them."

We cannot do better to close this chapter than by giving the prayer of the godly Baxter:—"O most glorious and gracious Creator and Redeemer, I humbly return my unfeigned thanks for the unspeakable mercies which I have received on Thy Day; and much more, for so great a mercy to all Thy churches and the world: and craving the pardon of the sins which I have committed on Thy Day, I beseech Thee to continue this exceeding mercy to Thy churches and to me, that its blessed privileges and comforts may not be forfeited and lost; and let me serve Thee in the life and light and love of Thy Spirit in these Thy holy days on earth, till I be prepared for and received into the everlasting rest in heavenly glory. Amen."

ITS OPPOSITION We now turn to the least pleasant part of our subject and contemplate the attacks which have been made upon this Divine ordinance. It has been fiercely assailed both in doctrine and in practice, and this by the professed friends of the Lord as well as by His open enemies. Yet this should not surprise us, for since the carnal mind is enmity against God, that enmity ever manifests itself against whatever is of His special ordering—and the more so in proportion as His honour and glory are bound up with any particular appointment. It is at just such a point that the hostility of Satan rages most furiously, seeking with all his might and arts to stir up his subjects to overthrow the same, knowing full well that if that can be accomplished his own evil cause will be greatly furthered and the kingdom of darkness more firmly established in the world.

Just as in carnal warfare there are certain strategic centers—"key positions"—on which the security of the whole "line" depends, and just as such a strategic center is made the "military objective" by the opposing army, who are determined to capture it at all costs, so it is in connection with the great forces of good and evil. There are certain bulwarks (Isa. 48:12, 13) which are of vital importance, the maintaining of which is essential for the furtherance of true piety, for once they be captured the way is wide open for the hordes of wickedness to wreak their evil will. Such a "bulwark" is the Sabbath: on the strict observance of it depends the well-being of Church and State alike. To keep the Sabbath Day holy secures the blessing of the Most High, but the desecration thereof most assuredly calls down His curse upon a land and people.

After what has been pointed out, there is little need now for us to enter upon a lengthy proof that the Holy Sabbath is one of the principal bulwarks of Zion. Or that it constitutes one of the most vital of all "strategic centers" in the defenses of Truth and godliness, spirituality and morality. It is like a mighty fortress which guards the entrance to a pass that gives access to a vast industrial center: once that fortress be captured the millions of people living behind it in the cities are then at the mercy of the advancing foe. And just as in a military campaign the attacking general makes the demolition of that fortress his main aim, concentrating the strength of his forces against it, so it is in connection with Satan's fight against the kingdom of God upon earth: he knows full well that the overthrow of the Sabbath would mean for him a "major victory."

To employ a rather different figure. The blessings which God has promised unto men—blessings both temporal and spiritual—flow most freely along the particular channels which He has Himself appointed. Contrariwise, if those channels be forsaken, then the blessings will also be forfeited. Now since the Sabbath is the day which the Lord has set apart for the communication of special blessing, then it is obvious that those blessings will be enjoyed in greatest measure by those who are the sincerest and strictest in its sacred observance. This is a fact which is capable of the clearest verification. Organized Christianity has been here for 1,900 years and during that lengthy span it has experienced many vicissitudes, passing through periods of prosperity on the one hand and of adversity on the other, of light and purity and darkness and impurity, of spiritual energy and of spiritual torpor.

Now it can be plainly shown from the chronicles of history that there has been to a very striking degree an unmistakable correspondence in those periods between the observance of Sabbath sanctity and the spiritual prosperity of the churches on the one hand and the neglect of the Sabbath's sanctity and spiritual declension of the churches on the other. In this we may also see parallels with the varied experiences of the nation of Israel in Old Testament times. While it is true that only fragments have survived the flight of time of what was recorded in the first two or three centuries A.D., yet sufficient is extant to show that in those centuries the Lord's Day was faithfully kept by His people in caves and catacombs, surrounded by every form of peril—as witness the testimonies of Eusebius, Justin Martyr, Tertullian, etc. How far, then, was the state of the Church a flourishing one in those early days?

In seeking the answer to our last question it must be distinctly borne in mind that the prosperity of Christianity is not to be gauged by the esteem in which it is held by the world in general. Very much to the contrary. "If ye were of the world, the world would love his own; but because ye are not of the world, but I have chosen you out of the world, therefore the world hateth you" (John 15:19). Unless that Divine pronouncement be held steadily before us we are certain to arrive at an entirely wrong answer to our inquiry. The world's hatred and opposition and not the world's love and co-operation is the surest index to the spiritual prosperity of Christianity. What the early Christians suffered at the hands of Nero and others of the Roman emperors which followed him, is too well known to need any description of ours. Thousands of Christ's followers sealed their testimony with their blood, yet despite the fierce persecution encountered, the Gospel continued to be diffused far and wide.

During the course of time Satan has resorted to a great variety of tactics in his efforts to stamp out the observance of the Sabbath, employing widely different measures and methods in his determination to choke this channel of Divine blessing. He employed a strange but effective instrument in his first onslaught. The fidelity and courage of the first martyrs evoked the deep esteem of the suffering but prospering Church. But alas—such is man—the praising of the martyrs soon took the place of the praising of Him who had sustained them, and ere long the places where they had suffered and the graves in which their mangled remains had been interred began to be regarded with superstitious veneration. It was not long until the days on which they had been martyred were regarded as comparatively sacred for their memories and were set apart as holy festivals hallowed by their death.

Not only were the virtues of the martyrs eulogized, but gradually it became popular to offer up prayers—at first for the souls of these Christians heroes, and later to the martyrs themselves as to a species of subordinate mediators. The efforts of the Enemy proved only too successful: the calendar of the Church soon became so filled with these "saints" days that the solitary dignity of the Lord's Day was crowded out and thus the channel of Divine blessing was choked. That holy veneration which had been accorded unto the Sabbath alone was now divided and extended to a multitude of human appointments, and even before the power of pagan Rome to suppress the public observance of the Christian Sabbath had passed away, its sole sanctity had disappeared before a legion of these spurious "holy days."

Constantine framed statutes requiring the inhabitants of cities to suspend their ordinary business and mechanics to abstain from their common labour on the Sabbath, and closed the courts of justice and all other public offices on that day—clear proof of how the early Church had been desirous to observe it. But the laws drawn up by this strange character who espoused Christianity introduced a most pernicious element: the Sabbath and the "holy festivals" of human invention were placed on the same level. The sequel may easily be imagined: those other "days" not being of Divine authority quickly degraded the sanctity of the Lord's Day from its sole supremacy over the consciences of the worshippers. An attempt to raise any human innovation in matters of religion to an equality with what is of Divine institution inevitably results in the lowering of the Divine and in the elevation of the human above the Divine.

What the Scriptures designate as "will worship" (Col. 2:23) is false worship, devised by the depraved heart of man to minister to his corrupt inclinations—under the pretence of exalted piety. Not only is this "will worship" a false one, but in proportion as it flourishes, true worship is defiled. From the days of Constantine onwards the progress of error and departure from the Truth went on with ever accelerating pace and power, until in a short time the whole year was overrun with saints' days and festivals and the Lord's Day was entirely set aside, or where it was still professedly regarded was degraded into one of recreation, amusement and festivities, of such kinds and degrees of debasement to be too sinful and shameful to describe.

It is needless to inquire whether or not the churches flourished spiritually during that time, for God cannot be mocked with impugnity. The fourth and fifth centuries A.D. witnessed a sad lowering of Christian standards: the Law was no longer faithfully enforced, the Gospel was grievously corrupted, and Worship became more and more paganized. It was not long ere a faithless Christendom was made to reap what it had sown, for the judgments of God ever fall upon the ecclesiastical sphere before they reach the civil (see 1 Peter 4:17). Where the Truth is rejected professors are given up by God to believe a lie. The setting up of saints' days and the degradation of the Lord's Day paved the way for the rise of the great anti-Christian power. The Roman Catholic apostasy was both the fully developed offshoot of the evils to which we have alluded, as she was also suffered by God to assume dominion as a mark of His displeasure upon an adulterous generation.

The growth and domination of the Papacy supplied a vivid demonstration of the spiritual adversity and desolation which had overtaken Christendom, and rightly have the centuries which followed been designated "the Dark Ages." No longer was the Word of God preached to the people, no longer was the Sabbath Day kept holy, no longer was the simplicity of Christian worship observed. Priestcraft poisoned every spring and the Water of Life was no longer obtainable. And where was the true Church of Christ to be found during this dark season: for even then God left not Himself without true witnesses on earth. The answer is, among the Vaudois valleys of the Alps—among that poor and despised people known as the Waldensians. No sooner did the degenerate system of Popery rise to power than the humble dwellers of the Piedmont become distinguished for their firm adherence to the standards of primitive Christianity, refusing to adopt any other rule of faith than the written Word of God, and exemplifying its precepts in their daily walk to an extent that few have done since.

Those possessing any acquaintance of Church history are familiar with the tragic but glorious sequel. The rage of Rome knew no bounds against this people who witnessed so faithfully and valorously for Christ, many of whom were given the great honour of suffering severely even unto death rather than yield to the demands of the Mother of Harlots. Even though most of their writings perished in the devastating persecution which they experienced, by which Rome strove might and main to exterminate them root and branch, yet sufficient have survived to furnish proof that the Waldensian Christians were characterized by Sabbath observance. In "The Noble Lesson," of date about 1,100, there is not only a clear avowal of the binding nature of the Moral Law—and consequently of the Fourth Commandment—but an enunciation of an important principle which shows their conception of the relation of the Law to the Gospel: "Christ did not change it that it should be abrogated, but renewed it that it might be better kept."

In the Confession of Faith of the same Church, the feasts and vigils of saints are denounced as "an unspeakable abomination." In an "Exposition of the Commandments" the following occurs, "They that will keep and observe the Sabbath of Christians, that is to say, will sanctify the Day of the Lord, must be careful of four things. The first is to cease from all earthly and worldly labours: the second, not to sin; the third, not to be idle in regard to good works; and fourth, to do those things which are for the good of the soul." And in another Confession, drawn up at a later period, the following article appears: "That on Sundays we ought to cease from our worldly labours, through zeal for God, and love towards our servants, and that we may apply ourselves to hearing the Word of God." These notices are enough to prove that the Waldensian Church was definitely distinguished by its sacred observance of the Lord's Day.

And what was the religious prosperity of Christianity in the Alps in those perilous times? Most pertinent is such an inquiry after what we have affirmed above. But again we must be careful not to employ a wrong standard of measurement, as we are so liable to do in a day when it is very common to estimate values wrongly. That prosperity is not to be looked for in numbers, in social prestige, or in anything which is highly esteemed among men; but rather in those spiritual fruits which are to the praise of God, because produced by the gracious operations of His Spirit. If to endure persecution as good soldiers of Jesus Christ without murmuring; if to suffer the acutest afflictions without wavering; if to experience continual persecution with an invincible patience and victorious faith be the marks of spiritual well-being, then the Waldensian Church certainly flourished spiritually.

"If to continue steadfast through a long agony of centuries, glorifying God in the midst of the furnace of persecution, even when it was heated seven times, maintaining still imperishable life and heavenly hope triumphant over all, be religious prosperity, that Church in the wilderness was marvelously prosperous. And if, in the midst of all its fiery trials, to strive to its power, and beyond its power, to act as a missionary Church, not only upholding its own testimony to the Truth, but striving to diffuse around it that priceless blessing, thus both continuing and extending true Christianity in spite of all the deadly efforts of anti-Christian Rome be religious prosperity, the faithful and zealous Waldensian Church was gloriously prosperous.

"The teaching of that Church pervaded the south of France and became instrumental there in winning many souls to Christ. Its living truths ran along the Rhine, communicating spiritual life to numbers, and preparing a way for future Gospel progress. Bohemia caught some rays of the sacred light, which in later age became the day-spring of heavenly brightness to suffering martyrs. The distant British Isles obtained some powerful life-germs, destined in due time to put forth a mighty and growing energy, not only for the protection of the suffering of the Waldenses themselves, but for the diffusion of Gospel Truth throughout the world. Such was the religious prosperity of the Bible-loving and Lord's-Day keeping Waldensian Church; and no true Christian will deny that it was a kind and measure of prosperity which God alone could have given, and the world could not take away— the full amount and value of which only the Day to come will reveal" (W. M. Hetherington, to whom we are indebted for the above quotations).

Popery succeeded at length in well nigh wearing out the saints and exterminating all who had borne testimony against her pernicious errors. The Waldensian Church was almost wholly destroyed or silenced. A reformation was attempted in Bohemia, but it was ruthlessly suppressed. Long had the Scriptures been a sealed book, not only to the masses, but because of their gross ignorance, to many of the priests as well. There had ceased to be any Christian Sabbath in the sense of a holy rest in the lands where Romanism dominated. The Lord's Day had been degraded into a day of special recreation, amusement, public shows and exhibitions—in short, of anything and everything to the utmost possible degree distinct and remote from the very appearance of sacredness. Thus the Devil seemed to have triumphed completely.

But a mighty change was impending, one which made manifest the Lord's supremacy. As it is in the material world, so it is in the moral and spiritual realms. As the Creator has given to the sea His decree, saying, "Hitherto shalt thou come, but no further: and here shall thy proud waves be stayed" (Job 38:11), so as Governor of this world He has limited the triumphs of the wicked. In the early part of the 16th century Satan received a check from which his kingdom has never fully recovered to this day. Under the Reformation the distinctive truths and principles of Christianity were once more publicly proclaimed and anti-Christian errors and practices boldly denounced.

127

In our day there are few who perceive the immensity of the task which confronted the Reformers, the difficulties they had to overcome, or the perils to which they were exposed. Papal despotism had to be encountered in the very heyday of its pride and power. Her monstrous fictions, superstitions, and idolatrous rites had to be swept away before a true and pure Christianity could appear. The vital truths of Divine revelation had to be virtually re-discovered. First to be rescued and preached was the cardinal doctrine of justification by faith. Then the Bible had to be translated from the dead languages into the living tongues of many lands, and given to the people as the alone Standard of faith and sole Rule of character and conduct. Then came the tremendous task of rescuing the Lord's Day from the obscurity to which it had been consigned, when buried beneath the multitude of festival days of human invention.

The work of the Reformers was so vast, so difficult, and so arduous, and was executed under such unfavourable conditions that we need not be surprised if parts of it were not so well done as were others, or that they never themselves erred. Rather must we marvel and be thankful that so much good was accomplished under their instrumentality. In regard to the Lord's Day they failed to give a sufficiently clear and decisive exposition. While they rightly adopted the principle that the whole of the Old Testament economy was typical and had its fulfillment in the New Testament dispensation—thus disposing of the Romish figment of an official priesthood with sacrifices in the Christian Church—yet they misapplied the same principle in connection with the Sabbath. Or perhaps it would be more correct to say, they applied it in such a way as to fail in establishing the right foundations on which the sacred obligations of that day now rests.

While it is quite clear that the Reformers themselves contended for the necessity and obligation of the Christian Sabbath, maintaining the same in their own personal examples, yet it must also be admitted that they employed language and uttered sentiments which were only too susceptible of being perverted and misapplied. This in fact quickly took place, especially in the Lutheran churches. Never so sound doctrinally as the Calvinists, they soon became lax in their Sabbath observance. So much so was this the case that one reliable writer tells us, "To such a degree was this the case, that many pious men among the ministers of the Lutheran churches seem to have been in doubt whether the fierce wars which so long desolated Germany were to be regarded as the cause of the extreme Sabbath profanation which prevailed, or as judgments inflicted on the community on account of that profanation."

The most striking and extensive demonstration of the connection between Sabbath observance and religious prosperity was seen in the British Isles in the 17th century. All who are acquainted with the history of that period know that the Puritans were particularly distinguished by their strict adherence to the sacred rest of the Lord's Day. Nor was this characteristic confined either to the Scotts or to those who separated themselves from the Established Church, but pertained also to those who remained within her pale. It is not generally known that the Westminster Confession of Faith, which contains the strongest assertion of the Divine authority and inviolable sanctity of the Christian Sabbath ever produced, was framed by a body of about 120 divines of whom only four were Scottish and five were Independents—all the rest having received Episcopal ordination.

Now the very times when the sanctity of the Sabbath was most diligently maintained in England were those in which pure and spiritual religion was in its highest state of freedom and prosperity; and the men under whose instrumentality this obtained are the ones whose writings are still the most precious treasure of English religious literature. Never was the smile of Heaven more apparent, never did true piety flourish so extensively, never has the power of the Holy Spirit been so manifest since the days of the Apostles, yet never was a season of Divine blessing so abruptly terminated. As the restoration of Charles the Second marked the overthrow of English Puritanism, so it brought in a flood of licentiousness which soon swept over the country, for unregenerate courtiers and commoners united together in throwing odium on Sabbath observance as a product of Puritanical fanaticism.

The awful effects of widespread Sabbath desecration were soon evident, for the judgments of God fell heavily upon both the religious and social life of the nation. The first half of the 18th century was marked by the most awful errors in the pulpit, spiritual death in the pew, and infidelity and profligacy amongst the masses, who were only too glad to be freed from the righteous restraints which pious legislators had placed upon them. Once again Satan had won a notable victory. But not for long was he suffered to enjoy the spoils of the same. Under the fearless preaching of George Whitefield and his fellows, revival was granted and true godliness given fresh life, and the Lord's Day was once more restored unto its rightful place.

During the 19th century the great Enemy of God and man entered upon a new campaign, seeking to undermine the foundations of this Divine institution, attacking it from the doctrinal side. He blinded the minds of those who professed to be the ministers of Christ, and alleged champions of the Truth, causing many of them to believe that the Sabbath was obsolete, pertaining not to this dispensation—and leading others to suppose that the observance of the Sabbath in this Christian era is mainly a matter of individual option, and that a much wider latitude in what they term "Christian liberty" is now permissible. In consequence thereof, Satan succeeded in banishing all witness to the Sabbath from thousands of pulpits, and caused the standard to be grievously lowered in most of the remaining ones. This acted like a poisonous leaven, the effects from which spread widely, until the rank and file of church-goers had no conscience on the subject: so long as they attended service once or twice, they felt they had fully discharged the obligations of the Lord's Day.

Little sagacity is required to foretell the effect upon the masses of such a poisoning of the ministry. To use a military figure: the muzzling of the pulpit on this vital truth was like the silencing of the guns on a fortress. "Once its cannons are put out of action, the capture of the citadel quickly follows. When those who were looked up to as the expounders of the Divine Law discredited the Sabbath, then who was left to offer real resistance to godless politicians playing fast and loose with those statutes of the realm which had once been framed for the purpose of preventing Sabbath profanation? If the rank and file of professing Christians considered they had discharged the obligations of the Sabbath merely by attending one or two religious services on that day, then need we be surprised if the irreligious masses clamoured louder and louder for a "brighter Sunday" and that those in governmental authority more and more yielded to their demands!

We shall now consider some of the arguments made use of by those who have insisted that the Sabbath pertains not to this dispensation. First, it has been asserted that the Ten Commandments were never given to anyone but the Jews. Such a postulate is most absurd. If the Moral Law be not binding upon Gentiles, then by what standard will God judge them? "Where no law is, there is no transgression" (Rom. 4:15). The erroneousness of such a postulate is made clearly manifest by, "Now we know that what things soever the Law saith, it saith to them who are under the Law: that every mouth may be stopped, and all the world may become guilty before God" (Rom. 3:19). Nothing could be plainer than that: the whole human race is "under the Law" and every member of it is brought in guilty by the same.

Second, it has been asserted that, whatever be the status and state of the unregenerate, yet Christians are "not under the Law, but under grace"

(Rom. 6:14). We must not here be misled by the mere sound of words. We must realize their sense—that the believer is no longer "under the Law" as a Covenant of Works, nor is he any more under its awful curse and condemnation—but as 1 Corinthians 9:21 definitely declares, he is "under the Law to Christ"—under it as a Rule of conduct. The Christian is required to "so walk even as He (the Lord Jesus) walked" (1 John 2:6), and Christ ever walked in perfect accord with the Moral Law (Psa. 40:8). The Holy Spirit has been given to the Christian for the express purpose of enabling him therein, the love of God being shed abroad in his heart for its fulfillment (Rom. 5:8 and 13:8-10).

It has been objected by others that the Sabbath precept in the Old Testament was entirely of a typical and ceremonial nature, looking forward to that spiritual rest which Christ should provide, and that when the substance was brought in, the shadow was done away. But were that the case, then the Moral Law consists of only nine and not "Ten Commandments" as Deuteronomy 4:13 specifically declares. The very fact that the Sabbath statute was incorporated into the Decalogue unequivocally denotes its essential moral character, and therefore, its lasting nature—the Fourth Commandment was, like the other nine, written by the finger of Jehovah upon the tables of stone, but no part of the ceremonial law was. Moreover, the Sabbath was instituted long before any part of the ceremonial law was given to Israel, before there were any types or shadows, before any promise of Christ was made. The Sabbath was appointed in Eden before the Fall, before there was any need for sacrifices!

Appeal has been made unto Galatians 4:10, 11 by those who are determined to banish the Sabbath from this dispensation: "Ye observe days and months and times and years. I am afraid of you, lest I have bestowed upon you labour in vain." The reference there is to the Judaising of the Galatian saints—to their being brought under bondage to the ceremonial law of Israel. False teachers had gone so far as to insist they must be circumcised in order to salvation: see Galatians 5:2, 6; 6:15. The "days" and "months" were those connected with the Jewish festivals, which were now obsolete: the very fact that the Holy Spirit here designated them, "the weak and beggarly elements" (Gal. 4:9) is clear proof that the Christian Sabbath was not there included, for it could never be described in such a way.

Appeal has also been made to, "Let no man therefore judge you in meat or in drink, or in respect of a holy day or of the new moon, or of the Sabbath days" (Col. 2:16). This is the favourite verse of those who insist that the Sabbath is not binding on Christians. That they refer to such a passage shows how untenable is their position. The Greek word here for "Sabbath" is in the plural number (as the translators denoted by adding "days" in italics), which intimates it is not the weekly Sabbath or the Moral Law that is in view. Moreover, there is no definite article before "Sabbaths," which is proof positive that the weekly Sabbath was not before the Apostle's mind. It was to things connected with the ceremonial law against which the Colossians were being warned, as the "meat," "drink," and "new moon" show.

Some have raised a silly objection drawn from the difference made by the meridian, from which it is argued it is impossible that all men could observe precisely the same day, and therefore God never intended they should. Now if men sailing either eastward or westward did not continually have seven days succeeding one another there would be some force in this trifle, but since the Sabbath statute simply requires from men one seventh of their time, or a seventh day, separated unto God and sanctified to His service, the objection is quite pointless. That the observance of this rest day should in all parts of the earth begin and end at the same minute, the Scriptures nowhere enjoin nor does the creation of God permit. It is sufficient that whether living in the northern or the southern hemisphere that all men observe the same proportion of time.

After all our articles on the Christianization of the Sabbath, especially the exposition of Hebrews 4:8-10, there is little need for us to refute seriatim the errors of those who insist that the Sabbath should, even now, be kept on Saturday rather than Sunday. The essential feature to be noted is that God requires us to set apart one seventh of our time and consecrate the same unto His worship. Nowhere in the Scriptures is it specified that the Lord ever commanded any people to observe the seventh day of the week—rather six days of work (without defining which days) followed by one of rest. Nor does the transference of the Sabbath from Saturday to Sunday involve any alteration in the Law, but merely a change in its administration.

It is true that the Apostles for a season, while their ministry had a special regard for the Jews (Rom. 1:16), for the conversion of that remnant among them according to the election of grace, went frequently into their synagogues on the seventh day to preach the Gospel (Acts 13:14; 16:13, etc). Yet it is evident they did so only to take opportunity of their assemblies, that they might preach to greater numbers of them, and that at a time when they were prepared to attend unto sacred things. Upon the same ground and for the same reason we find Paul endeavouring to be at Jerusalem at the feast of Pentecost (Acts 20:16). But we nowhere read that Christians at any time assembled together on the seventh day for the worship of God.

And now our task is completed, very imperfectly so, we are fully conscious. But if the Lord is pleased to own these feeble efforts unto a stirring up of His people for a stricter observing of this Divine ordinance and in using their influence to protest against its awful profanation, we shall not have laboured in vain.

"A Sabbath well spent brings a week of content,

And strength for the toils of the morrow:

But a Sabbath profaned, whate'er may be gained,

Is a certain forerunner of sorrow."

Look For Other Books Published By:

Classic Domain Publishing

NOTE: The books from *Classic Domain Publishing* are intended to awaken people – Christians, Backsliders, and Non-Christians alike - to the urgency of seeking Christ in order to make the rapture or to make it to heaven if they should die before the rapture. Most of the books by *Classic Domain Publishing* are Public Domain and are "re-published" in order to make the books more readily available to the modern era in the *"Last Minutes"* of these *"Last Days."*

If there are other Public Domain books that have changed your life, please let me know so that we can perhaps list it or publish it as a "life changing" book.

Contact me by email at:

peralta_mike@hotmail.com

Other Life Changing Works

(List below by Mike Peralta – Chief Editor of Classic Domain Publishing)

The Bible both Old and New Testament. The best book as God never lies and He is never mistaken.

"Hell Testimonies" by Mike Peralta. This is a compilation of several Hell Testimonies from several people around the world. In my opinion this is the best book, after the Bible, (not because I'm the author) but because it mentions many types of sins that will send you to Hell. Some of the sins mentioned will probably hit home to you as you read this book. This book has helped me truly repent of sin more than any other book.

"While Out Of My Body I Saw God, Hell, and the Living Dead" by Dr. Roger Mills. This is a superb book about Hell. Jesus explains some things about Hell and sin that I have never read anywhere else. However, as far as I can see, it is all consistent with what the bible says.

"A Divine Revelation of Hell" by Mary Kathryn Baxter. This book shows in graphic detail what torment people in Hell are suffering. This book has been read by many and has helped many repent from their sins and obey God in their lives.

"Heaven Is So Real" by Choo Thomas. This book discusses both Heaven and Hell and reveals a great deal about the love and personality that Jesus has to His children as evidenced by how Jesus interacts with

Choo Thomas. With a tenderness and friendly and loving and compassionate heart, you will learn the character and demeanor of Jesus through this book.

"Backsliding to Hell" by Mike Peralta. This book is written to help the backslider or those who are sinning after receiving Jesus in the past. It clearly explains through the Bible that the backslider will definitely go to Hell unless he or she repents of their sinning and turns back to Jesus. At first, to avoid promoting myself, I was not going to include this in my list of life changing books (truth2.weebly.com) but the Holy Spirit insisted that I include this book, so it must be even more important than I, myself, realize.

Rapture and Tribulation books by Susan Davis: "Bride of Christ Prepare Now", "Left Behind After The Rapture", "Rapture or Tribulation", "Marriage Supper of the Lamb", "I Am Coming (Volumes 1 to 6)" by Susan Davis and Sabrina De Muynck. These rapture books are prophetic messages from Jesus to help prepare the Bride of Christ (Christ's true church) on how to prepare for the very soon rapture. It clearly shows that those who are not ready and are not looking to Jesus' soon coming will be left behind to face the anti-christ and certain death at the hands of the most ruthless evil dictator that will take power and world domination after the rapture. Also near the time of the rapture there will many deaths and those who are not ready will end up in Hell.

"Final Call, Exodus, My Son David, True Maturity" by Deborah Melissa Moller (Four Book Series). This four part series (combined in one book) has helped me more than any other book to get close to Jesus and obey God's will. It is like Jesus is personally teaching me how to follow Him, obey Him, love Him, and to do the Father's will. This is an extremely valuable book. It is truly a *Pearl of Great Price*. It is provided by Jesus to prepare His Bride for the very soon rapture.

Links to rapture books are also at: truth2.weebly.com

I urge you to read all these books – especially the Bible – over and over again. There is extremely little time left to get right with God. Jesus is returning much sooner than you think and there is soon to be terrible judgments on earth.

Surrender your life completely to Jesus now.

It is extremely and eternally dangerous to delay your full and absolute commitment to Christ. It doesn't matter what anyone else tells you – they cannot help you when you end up in Hell. Trust only God. Of course, love and pray for everyone – but trust only God.

Seek Him with all your being now before it's too late.

Feel free to email me at:

peralta_mike@hotmail.com

49689761R00079

Made in the USA
Lexington, KY
20 February 2016